The Theory and Interpretation of Narrative Series

Having a Good Cry:
Effeminate Feelings and Pop-Culture Forms

Robyn R. Warhol

The Ohio State University Press
Columbus

Library of Congress Cataloging-in-Publication Data

Warhol, Robyn R.
Having a good cry: effeminate feelings and pop-culture forms / Robyn
R. Warhol.
p. cm. — (The theory and interpretation of narrative series)
Includes bibliographical references and index.
ISBN 0-8142-0928-9 (hardcover : alk. paper) — ISBN 0-8142-5108-0
(pbk. : alk. paper) — ISBN 0-8142-9011-6 (CD-ROM)
1. Women and literature. 2. Television and women. 3.
Women—Psychology. 4. Emotions. I. Title. II. Series.
PN56.5.W64 W375 2002
809'.89287—dc21
2002013495

Cover design by Dan O'Dair
Printed by Thomson-Shore Inc.

9 8 7 6 5 4 3 2 1

For Seth

Contents

Preface:
Six Readers Reading—and Feeling

Reading is a physical act. Depending on how you look at it, reading is also a cognitive activity, a psychological process, a political engagement, an intertextual encounter, an aesthetic exercise, an academic discipline, a communitarian endeavor, a spiritual practice, a habit. But whatever else it may entail, reading always happens in and to a body. What is the somatic experience of taking in a narrative text? How does reading feel?

This question has been asked so seldom, hardly any literary-critical language exists for answering it. Novelists and poets are adept at describing the physical manifestations of emotional reaction—the subtle and dramatic contortions of facial features, the flexing and flaccidity of muscles, the sensations in skin and bone and internal organs generated by "feelings." Sometimes literary authors even articulate the bodily reactions they have to other authors' texts, as when A. E. Housman averred that "Poetry indeed seems to me more physical than intellectual. . . . Experience has taught me, when I am shaving of a morning, to keep watch over my thoughts, because, if a line of poetry strays into my memory, my skin bristles so that the razor ceases to act. This particular symptom is accompanied by a shiver down the spine; there is another which consists in a constriction of the throat and a precipitation of water to the eyes" (193). Housman might not have put it this way, but that tightness in the throat and wetness in the eye are the prelude to "having a good cry."

Literary theorists and critics, unlike poets and novelists, do not often get beyond abstract categories in discussing "reader response." We talk so little about the affects reading generates in our bodies, we are hardly aware of their repeated, familiar existence. In conversations and correspondence with colleagues, students, and friends over the past ten years, I have tried to push them into consciousness of their bodily reactions to the genres they habitually read, as I have tried to find literary-theoretical formulations of those reactions. The following vignettes reveal my most responsive interlocutors' best efforts at describing what reading feels like. Pulling against abstractions like "I was moved" or "I felt great," these accounts reflect avid readers' own reports of what their bodies do when they are reading. As each vignette inevitably reveals the strain of trying to articulate the somatic experience of reading, it indicates the purpose of this book: to find a language for talking about the reader's body.

1

A woman in her late twenties reflects on her physical reactions to reading a Dickens novel for a graduate course where it has been assigned in serial parts: "I've had some out-loud chuckles, and some occasions of my eyes opening wider, or maybe it's my eyebrow rising when something surprising happens." She reports a feeling of "shock" at an unexpected twist in the plot: "I had a distinct physical response—kind of a sigh or a change in my breathing. I looked up from the page even though there was no one in the room to share the experience with; I think I smiled, too."[1] The act of reading registers in her lungs, rib cage, and pectoral muscles with that change in her breathing; it registers on her face as well: if no one sees her upturned lips, her raised eyebrow, her widened eyes, she feels them just the same. Even if she were somehow to experience no emotional turbulence outside of her reading of books, a lifetime of such surprises would etch lines in her now-smooth forehead; the repeated smile would leave tiny lines at the edges of her mouth and in that space where the skin is particularly thin, between the corner of her eye and her cheekbone.

2

A longtime viewer of a daily soap opera, *As the World Turns,* watches a videotaped episode as he has done continually for more than a decade, since his early thirties. He tunes in reluctantly this time, still sore from the recent (as it turned out, temporary) departure of his favorite actress, Elizabeth Hubbard, whom he feels has made this serial worth watching for so many years. Taking advantage of the time-shifting his VCR makes possible, he scans for the scenes that might pique his interest. As he watches, he feels angry, missing Hubbard's presence and resenting the proliferation of "cast members who couldn't act their way out of a paper bag." He pouts, smirks, and rolls his eyes. His anger shades into contempt—his smirk gives way to a curled lip—which shades into boredom, experienced as physical and mental restlessness: "While I'm watching," he reports, "I'm also flipping through the pages of a magazine, eating, staring out the window, wondering whether I should go buy a shirt, etc."

    The boredom, though, does not signify an absence of feelings: as the viewer puts it, "This boredom and distraction are inseparable from a certain low-level anxiety: a sense that I'm wasting my time, an eagerness for the scene I'm watching to be over, even a vague, pathetic hope that, somehow, Elizabeth Hubbard will appear again, as though her firing and departure were all just a bad dream." (Given the propensity of television serials to write off bad story line decisions in just this way, the anxious viewer's hope, "vague and pathetic" though it may be, is hardly unrealistic.) The vague hope phases into a sense of hurt, "a sense that, along with Hubbard, I myself had been fired by the show—more or less violently excluded from its imagined audience," which makes the viewer feel still more anger—more pouting, more eye rolling, more smirking.

The viewer's eyes have something else to do, though, besides rolling with disdain. He admits that "finally, emerging out of a mild curiosity as to how the show has changed since I in effect said, 'You can't fire me, I quit!'" he feels "an equally mild interest in the new male personnel—in particular, a new 'hunk' somehow associated with Julia. I thought at first he might be a recast Jack, but no, it's another generic gym bunny, whom I size up in the usual way—eyes vaguely cruising face and body, then, seeing nothing special, moving on to the next object, in this case, the ridiculously dated haircut" of another recently recast male character. The curiosity and the interest are only mild; the sizing up reveals nothing special. "And so," concludes this wry viewer, "with the late Anthony Newley, I cry, 'Stop the world, I want to get off!'"

The viewer records this series of sensations as an example of how he typically feels while watching "his soap." Dissatisfied as he seems, he will almost certainly tune in again; the globe spinning in space that has served for decades as this soap's logo has not made its last turn on his television screen. The anger, the hope, the contempt, the hurt, the distraction, the anxiety, and even the boredom are as much a part of his customary viewing as the mild curiosity and the equally mild interest in maybe seeing something special, maybe even Elizabeth Hubbard or some really compelling hunk, someone worth looking at. The pout, the curled lip, the smirk, the rolled eye are all part of the habit: they map his body's participation in his daily reading of the soap.

3

Asked to reflect in a journal entry on what reading novels feels like, a graduate student describes what his body experiences when he is reading:

> I gnaw nervously on my fingernails when I read something that interests me. Along with nibbling, I also shift about in my seat as if trying to get comfortable when I am really interested in the book. That actually annoys me quite a bit because I have a nice comfortable chair that I sit in. Along with the above reactions, I also wiggle my legs and feet when the plot becomes particularly juicy.

xii   Preface

> The reactions I have when I am not interested in the reading are quite different. I yawn a lot. As I get more and more bored with the reading I tend to slink [*sic*] lower and lower in the chair, usually putting the footrest up and leaning back. Often when I am interested I'll find myself sitting up cross-legged and leaning forward into the book.

The shifting and wiggling leave their marks—however subtle—in the muscles of his legs and feet, just as his movements will eventually mark his nice comfortable chair; "slinking lower" into that chair and "leaning forward into the book," repeated over and over throughout years of avid reading, will have distinctly different long-term effects on the condition of his lower back.

This man's account of his reading posture recalls the address to the "reader" in the opening passages of Italo Calvino's *If on a Winter's Night a Traveler:*

> Find the most comfortable position: seated, stretched out, curled up, or lying flat. Flat on your back, on your side, on your stomach. In an easy chair, on the sofa, in the rocker, the deck chair, on the hassock. In the hammock, if you have a hammock. On top of your bed, of course, or in the bed. You can even stand on your hands, head down, in the yoga position. With the book upside down, naturally. Of course, the ideal position for reading is something you can never find. . . . Well, what are you waiting for? Stretch your legs, go ahead and put your feet on a cushion, on two cushions, on the arms of the sofa, on the wings of the chair, on the coffee table, on the desk, on the piano, on the globe. Take your shoes off first. If you want to, put your feet up; if not, put them back. . . .
>
> You are at your desk, you have set the book among your business papers as if by chance; at a certain moment you shift a file and you find the book before your eyes, you open it absently, you rest your elbows on the desk, you rest your temples against your hands, curled into fists, you seem to be concentrating on an examination of the papers and instead you are exploring the first pages of the novel. Gradually you settle back in the chair, you raise the book to the level of your nose, you tilt the chair, poised on its rear legs, you pull out a side drawer of the desk to prop your feet on it; the position of the feet during reading is of maximum importance, you stretch your legs out on the top of the desk, on the files to be expedited. (3, 7)

Among these teasing directives to his fictitious narratee, Calvino includes hints that might make his actual readers self-conscious not only about their own physical postures as they hold the book, but about exigencies of the body that can interfere with the physical demands of reading: "Try to foresee now everything that might make you interrupt your reading. Cigarettes within reach, if you smoke, and the ashtray. Anything else? Do you have to pee? All right, you know best" (4).

4

Very few professional literary critics have written with anything like Calvino's level of self-consciousness about their bodies' implication in the act of reading, but D. A. Miller (1988) is in this respect, as in so many, exceptional. His account of "our reading bodies'" encounter with Victorian sensation novels, for example, emphasizes the genre's "characteristic adrenaline effects: accelerated heart rate and respiration, increased blood pressure, the pallor resulting from vasoconstriction, and so on" (*The Novel and the Police,* 146). These are the bodily fight-or-flight reactions familiar to devotees of horror fiction, thrillers, and action adventures, as well as sensation novels.

Delineating the physical impact a sensation novel might have on a susceptible reader, Miller argues that feelings—in the culture that produces and receives such texts—are never gender-neutral. According to his subtly detailed reading of Wilkie Collins's *The Woman in White,* "we 'catch' sensation from the neuropathic body of the Woman who, no longer confined or controlled in an asylum, is free to make our bodies resonate with—like—hers" (153):

> Every reader is consequently implied to be a version or extension of the Woman in White, a fact that entails particularly interesting consequences when the reader is—as the text explicitly assumes he is—male. . . . His excitements come from—become—her nervous excitability; his rib cage, arithmetically Adam's, houses a woman's quickened respiration, and his heart beats to her skittish rhythm; even his pallor (which of course he cannot see) is mirrored back to him only as hers, the Woman in White's. (153–54)

Characteristically, Miller turns his discussion to the implications this raises for the sexual identity of the male reader who finds his body invaded, as it were, by all these feminine sensations. Given the emphasis of Miller's project, this turn from discussing gender to talking about sexuality makes sense. Backing up to look more closely at the physical sensations he describes, however, we might note that they are not specifically sexual feelings: the rib cage moving with rapid breaths, the heart beating to a skittish rhythm, the pallor of the facial skin might be read metonymical-ly as referring to the Woman's or the reader's bodily sexual functions, but in themselves they are physical affects that are not distinctly or exclusive-ly sexual. If not necessarily sexual, they are, nevertheless—as Miller asserts—strongly gendered: gendered feminine, in this case, as the reader who feels with, through, and for the Woman in White is manifesting the Woman's sensations in his or her own body, be it male or female. Miller does not invoke it, but the term in common circulation for describing manifestations of "femininity" in a male body is "effeminacy." As my Introduction will explain, I embrace this term with reference to signs of feminine feeling in male and female bodies alike.

If Miller's description of the gendered reading body steers clear not just of effeminacy, but also of the first-person singular, his essay's coda renders his own male rib cage—"arithmetically Adam's"—vividly present in his text. In what he calls a "note on the author's body," Miller reports that "shortly after I began writing this essay, the muscles on my shoulders and back went into spasm," due to a displaced rib that he understands as a hysterical disorder intricately interconnected with reading and writing about Collins's text. "Now that a practiced hand has put the fugitive rib back into its cage," Miller comments, "my spine tingles to have borne out my assumption of that 'nonrecognition' which evidently also obtains between the somatics of writing and what is written about" (191). He ends on a confession of feeling "too mute to do more than designate the crucial task of identifying in this writing the equivocal places where 'sen-sation' has gone, not to say love" (191). Indeed, where the sensations born of reading go—beyond those facial lines and back problems I have been invoking—is an important question to pursue, if we are to understand the process by which bodies are invested with gender.

5

A lawyer verging on forty sits by himself at a first-run screening of Steven Spielberg's *Saving Private Ryan.* His wife has asserted the effeminate pre-rogative of flinching from a notoriously violent movie, and has refused to see it; his children, only newly adolescent, are too young to have come along with him to this celebrated but R-rated film. He notices that other people in the theater, including some teenage girls sitting behind him, are seated in the same posture he has assumed: slouched down in their seats, with their feet up on the backs of the chairs ahead of them and their knees in their faces. His body is comfortable this way—it is his characteristic posture when he is alone in his office, chatting on the telephone.

Now he is not talking. He is concentrating on the film, and on how it is making him feel. Absorbed in what he experiences as the film's "intensity," he has been completely taken in by Spielberg's camera, which has zoomed in on the eyeball of an aged World War II veteran visiting a military graveyard, then zoomed out to suggest that the eye belongs to the Tom Hanks character, through whose point of view he understands the subsequent scenes to be focalized. This gives the viewer confidence that Hanks's character will survive the many bloody episodes that make up the narrative; the sense of confidence has a calming effect on his agitation, whenever Hanks's character faces imminent danger.

The lawyer is moved by the violent action. He surprises himself with the depth of his gratification at seeing representations of German soldiers being killed. He thinks of this as "just what the movie wants you to want," and he connects it with an attitude he recognizes as nostalgia for something he never experienced directly, but knows only through popular-cultural formulations of a patriotic past, "the last time we all were together, behind one thing, fighting evil—it's a tremendous feeling!" His excitement during the penultimate scene—where Hanks's mission to rescue Matt Damon's character, Private Ryan, is accomplished—culminates in a strongly felt surprise when the Hanks character is killed, proving the viewer's sense of confidence in the outcome to have been false: that old man's eye on which Spielberg's camera trick pivots belongs to Private Ryan, after all.

As the scene flashes forward again, and an aged Matt Damon—agonizing over whether his life has adequately compensated Tom Hanks's sacrifice—sobs over the military grave, the lawyer feels himself beginning to cry. Crying is something he says he almost never does "in real life," though it happens sometimes while he reads touching passages from children's books aloud to his family. A wave of sensation wells up from behind his breastbone to someplace in his head; his eyes begin to water, and if anyone were to speak to him, his voice would crack in answering, because of the tightness in his throat. As he is among strangers, he need not speak. He takes no pains to conceal his tears, because the signs of his crying are so faint, no one would see them. Especially in this darkened theater, he runs no risk of appearing effeminate.

6

I am in a small, crowded theater on a subzero Saturday night in downtown Burlington, Vermont, watching *Wag the Dog* for the first time; the audience is appreciative, though I notice I am the only one laughing at some of the jokes about Los Angeles. The film's script—cowritten by David Mamet and just as cynical, rapid-fire, and ironic as I expect his work to be—speaks to many of my current preoccupations with pop culture and its formulas.

The movie's premise is that you can distract the U.S. public from a White House sex scandal by fabricating reports of a war in "some obscure country" like Albania. The film suggests that if you mobilize the appropriate technologies of feeling—including news footage (such as the computer-enhanced, entirely fictive video of the young girl running from a burning village, clutching a stricken-looking cat, which is actually a bag of Tostitos before the computer makes the substitution); pop songs (such as the "feel-good" patriotic song sounding just like "We Are the World, We Are the Children," the pseudo-military pop anthem deploying the rhythms and harmonies of "The Ballad of the Green Berets," and the authentic-sounding imitation of a 1930s blues number called "Good Old Shoe," complete with the hisses and pops of an aged vinyl record); and popular fads (like the one, dreamed up by a professional "Fad King," that involves throwing old tennis shoes over power lines and into trees)—you can make U.S. audiences feel whatever you want them to feel.

The film's point could not be more explicit. When the fictional U.S. president objects to a speech he must read on the grounds that it is "too corny," his handlers ask that thirty "secretaries" be gathered in the oval office for a trial reading of the speech. Once Dustin Hoffman—as the Hollywood producer called in to help the president through this crisis of image—has finished performing the speech, every one of the secretaries (all of them women, not coincidentally) is sobbing, even though the speech makes no reference to anything real or true within the world of the story. Following this strategy, the president will be reelected despite the sex scandal. Of course the speech is "too corny," the film suggests, and of course it *works*. Every one of those secretaries is having a good cry.

As I watch the film, I am thinking hard about the parallels between its thesis and the arguments I have recently been developing: certain pop-culture formulas can be astonishingly effective in evoking predictable patterns of feeling, even (perhaps especially) when their origins are the very antithesis of authenticity. I have been thinking about these formulas, about how texts make audiences cry, since the movie began—really, I have been thinking about these formulas for ten years. I ought to be immune to the kind of manipulations the film depicts, if a critical awareness of formulaic effects is any defense against their power over audiences.

And then something happens that astonishes me. The moment in the story comes when the president's PR advisors are revealing their plan for focusing public sentiment once the "war" has been officially declared not to exist. They show a mug shot of an American "prisoner of war" in Albania, allegedly being held by fictitious Albanian terrorists. The face is Woody Harrelson's, carrying all the intertextual connotations of both his moronically sunny, harmless persona on *Cheers* and the pathologically dark murderer he has more recently played in *Natural Born Killers:* the feelings this face invokes in the viewer familiar with Hollywood idioms could go either way, to sentimentality or to terror. The pained, morose expression on the face and the body's pose deploy the semiotics of prisoner-of-war photos from the latter part of the twentieth century. The photo shows Harrelson wearing a sweater with rips in the front which the commentators, in voice-over, reveal to be a message in Morse code. The commentators interpret the message: it reads, "Courage, Mom."

"Courage, Mom." The phrase floats from the Dolby speakers into the theater, and I feel a familiar burning in the back of my throat, a momentary clutch of the muscles behind my palate, a tingling in the sinuses along my cheekbones; suddenly my eyes begin to sting as they fill with tears. "Courage, Mom." There is nothing authentic, nothing genuine, nothing "real" about the moment, nothing in the diegetic context that could explain my reaction: the film's multiple ironies add layers to the defenses my academic study of sentimentalism should have established for me years ago. And yet the tears roll out from under my glasses and down my cheeks, requiring me to wipe my eyes surreptitiously so that my husband, sitting next to me, will not see how easily, indeed how ludicrously, I can be made to cry. I am embarrassed because this crying has no foundation in my life experience, no reference point in any patriotic sentiments I might be supposed to harbor toward images of U.S. soldiers—I embrace no such sentiments. To be sure, I am a middle-aged, middle-class, white North American mother, and to that extent my identity is aligned with the "Mom" addressed in the Morse-coded message. But if my crying results from any association I am making between my three-year-old son and the image of Woody Harrelson on the screen, I can't see it. I recognize these tears as resulting not from a "real feeling," but from the mobilization of a familiar narrative formula, despite my best efforts (not to mention David Mamet's) to defuse that formula's power by analyzing and even ridiculing it. And yet, for me—and I assume for other viewers who habitually cry at the movies—something about the physical appeal of having a good cry transcends the film's cynicism and even my own.

If popular narratives deploy formulas to invoke predictable patterns of feeling in their devotees, what shapes do those patterns take? If audiences of thrillers and action-adventures experience again and again the pounding heart and pallor of the fight-or-flight reaction; if readers of long-running serial novels and viewers of soap opera continually oscillate between hope and curiosity on the one hand, boredom and annoyance on the other; if fans of marriage-plot films and novels and other forms of sentimental fiction repeatedly indulge in having a good cry, what traces of those affects will their bodies carry over the long term? Given that each of these genres carries strongly gendered connotations in the mainstream Anglo-American culture of the past hundred and fifty years, what is the relationship between these patterns of feeling in readers' bodies and the masculinity or femininity of those bodies? And how might the gender categories of "masculinity," "femininity," and "effeminacy" become more flexible, less prescriptive, less pejorative, and less rigidly tied to categories of sexual identity, as shifts in the construction and reception of these popular genres occur? In trying to answer these questions, I will investigate what the repeated experience of such formulaically induced feelings might mean for gendered subjectivity in nineteenth- and twentieth-century British and American mainstream culture.

Acknowledgments

When I was a first-year college student, one of my nineteen-year-old suite-mates took me to task in the dormitory bathroom for the way I used to apply my makeup and blow-dry my hair. "Don't open your eyes so wide when you're looking in the mirror," she cautioned, "because if you raise your eyebrows like that all the time, your forehead will get wrinkles." Although I tried for a while to follow her advice, today that seems to me to have been an unnecessary sacrifice of effeminate gesture in the interest of a goal that was, after all, unattainable: eventually all foreheads wrinkle. I am grateful to the many eye-rolling, gesticulating, eyebrow-raising, and (occasionally) crying colleagues and companions to whom I have gravitated since then, especially for their willingness to risk wrinkles every time they visibly emote while conversing. Without the community of supportive fellow-feeling they have formed for my own effeminate tendencies, I could not have done this writing. With gratitude and affection, I acknowledge them all.

I am first of all indebted to Jane Shattuc, who cotaught with me the course where the ideas for this book began, and with whom I first started to talk about *Having a Good Cry*. I owe equal thanks to Mary Lou Kete— my dear student, dear colleague, dear friend—who introduced me when she was a mere sophomore to melodramatic acting styles and who since that time has continually contributed more than anyone else to my understanding of what this project is about. I also thank Mary Lou and the other members of my writing groups—Helena Michie, Beth Kowaleski Wallace, and Irene Kacandes especially—for patient rereadings of constantly evolving (and, as Helena has called them, "weird-ass") arguments.

Long-running serial conversations about reading, feeling, and gender with Joe Litvak, with Roxanne Lin, and especially with Paul Van de Graaf have profoundly influenced my thinking. Their passion for reading is rivaled only by their generous willingness to talk about how it feels. I also remember useful and supportive comments on my work from Robyn Wiegman, Paul Morrison, Hilary Schor, Joe Childers, Mary Ann O'Farrell, Joanna Frueh, Andrew Miller, Doug Mao, Ellen Esrock, Susan Bernstein, Nancy Welch, Lisa Schnell, David Herman, Michael Stanton, Mercy Russell Hyde, Elizabeth Fenton, and Armistead Maupin. Each of them had something positive to say at a time when I really needed to hear it.

Students have enthusiastically contributed suggestions and accounts of experiences too numerous to detail. Among graduate students, I want particularly to thank Irene MacFarland, Katy Klutznik, and Tom Ford of the University of Vermont; Yoon Cho of the University of Southern California; and Chuck Jackson of Rice University. I am also deeply grateful to Dan Cone for help in manuscript preparation.

As series editors for Ohio State University Press, Peter Rabinowitz and Jim Phelan embodied my ideal readers, bestowing attention on my drafts that sometimes took my breath away and always improved my logic. Sue Lanser's beautifully trenchant review of the manuscript was—like all her readings—as challenging as it was transformative for me. Thomas Foster and the editorial board of *Genders* also provided influential feedback that shaped my thoughts on soap operas.

Tom Streeter generously read and listened to what often must have sounded goofy to his Birmingham-school, media-studies-trained ear, giving me many invaluable bibliographic suggestions and much-needed encouragement.

∞

Though nothing appears here in exactly its original form, parts of various chapters repeat material that I have published in journals and edited collections. Chapters 1 and 2 draw from "As You Stand, So You Feel and Are: The Crying Body and the 19th-Century Text," in *Tattoo, Torture, Mutilation, and Adornment: The De-Naturalization of the Body in Culture and Text,* edited by Fran Mascia-Lees and Patricia Sharpe (Albany: SUNY Press, 1992), 100–25. Chapter 1 also incorporates part of "Guilty Cravings: What Feminist Narratology Can Do for Cultural Studies," from *Narratologies: New Perspectives on Narrative Analysis,* edited by David Herman (Columbus: Ohio State University Press, 1999), 340–56. An expanded version of "How Narration Produces Affect: Femininity as Affect and Effect in *The Color Purple,*" *Narrative* 19, no. 2 (May 2001): 182–87, is included in chapter 2. An earlier version of chapter 5 appeared as "Feminine Intensities: Soap Opera-Viewing as a Technology of Gender" in *Genders,* no. 28 (1998) at http://www.genders.org. I thank these publishers for permission to reuse the materials.

My work on serial forms was supported by a National Endowment for the Humanities summer grant, as well as several bequests from the Dean's Fund of the College of Arts and Sciences at the University of Vermont. I am thankful to have had the time this money bought.

CHAPTER ONE

Introduction:
Effeminacy, Feelings, Forms

Gender and emotion, gendered affect, gender and genre, the gendered body, the reader's body, gender and narrative forms: the terminological territory of *Having a Good Cry* is familiar, but I propose to redraw the maps we have followed in linking up these topics in literary and cultural theory. Whereas "gender" often points critical discussions of the body in the direction of "sexuality," I turn away from that well-trodden path; while literary studies of readers' emotions usually indicate a psychoanalytic approach, I explore alternative topographies of the relationships between reading and feeling. My subtitle's keyword, "effeminacy," serves for me as a signpost for the swerve I am making away from gender theory's high road. I am claiming "effeminate" as a new honorific to refer positively to gendered—which is not necessarily or not only to say sexualized—traits of persons who do not meet culturally determined standards of "masculinity": gay, straight, and bisexual men and women alike. Each of the vignettes in my Preface describes a person experiencing different degrees of "effeminate" physical reactions to texts—crying, rolling the eyes, trembling, and smirking are not part of the generally received performance of masculine behavior. To call these reactions "feminine," though, is too easily to associate them exclusively with women—too easily, especially, from the point of view of the various men whose reading bodies I am examining along with the bodies of women readers. Recognizing that "effeminacy" not only shares "femininity's" pejorative connotations, but carries negative denotations as well, I begin by asking: what's wrong with having a good cry, anyway?

Typically, if a literary-critical project takes on the subject of the gendered body, it is safe to assume it will at least touch upon the topic of sexuality. The kind of move D. A. Miller (1988) makes in his reading of *The Woman in White,* from sex (the female character, the male reader) through gender (the feminine sensations evoked in and through those female and male bodies) to sexuality (the homosexuality implicit in the male reader's

1

bodily predicament) is characteristic not just of Miller's own work, but of the broader field of gender-centered theory and criticism in the 1990s. A glance at the "Gender Studies" section of any university press's catalogue shows that the term generally denotes studies of sexuality; anthologies of literary theory tend to categorize sexuality studies, gender studies, and feminist literary theory and criticism as interchangeable.[1] Fifteen years have passed since Gayle Rubin (1993) exhorted cultural theorists "to distinguish between gender, on the one hand, and erotic desire, on the other" (41); although she argued persuasively "that it is essential to separate gender and sexuality analytically to more accurately reflect their separate social existence" (42), the "definitional fusion" (43) between gender and sexuality that she perceived has not worn away.

What makes the separation "essential" is poststructuralist feminism's antiessentialist commitment to avoid jumping to conclusions about the sexual significances of gendered aspects of male and female bodies, to resist reading "feminine female" as indicating "heterosexual woman," or "masculine male" as meaning "straight man"—hence overlooking the range of feminine women and masculine men who identify as bisexual or as lesbian and gay—and to complicate the automatic association of "masculine woman" with "lesbian" or "feminine man" with "homosexual," thus taking into account those hetero- and bisexual persons whose gender performance transgresses what is assumed to be "natural" both to their sex and their sexuality. Given that one of academic feminism's chief goals through the 1990s was to dismantle essentializing models of gender, the tendency of "gender studies" to continue to blur into "sexuality studies" is surprising.[2]

I am interested in trying to move the conversation about gender and the body in a different direction for the present decade, to talk about gendered bodily experience—like crying, or like the physical manifestations of suspense, for example—that is not specifically sexual. My purpose is to try to take the next step in feminist theory's decades-long attempt to detach the "natural" connection between (bodily) sex and (cultural) gender. By "gender" I mean the styles, the looks, the moves, the gestures, the postures, the inflections, and the touches that mainstream American culture has enforced and reinforced as appropriate to women's bodies or to men's. The woman crying over a melodramatic film about a mother-and-child reunion is having a bodily experience that mainstream, contemporary U.S. culture configures as feminine, and also—in that her weeping suggests weakness—effeminate. In this instance, her sex is female, her gender feminine; at other moments or in other respects, she may have "masculine" traits—perhaps, when she leaves the movie, she goes back to a job (like Virginia Woolf's Chloe and Olivia) as a bench chemist; perhaps she habitually dresses in chinos and button-down shirts; perhaps she does not hesitate to assert herself in intellectual discussions; perhaps she enjoys going hunting. Her experience of crying at a film makes her gender, for this moment, feminine, but only for this moment, and not in any essential or eternal sense. And yet does this gendered gesture necessarily reveal anything about her sexuality? Does it suggest that she must be "gay" or "straight," or provide any clues to the sexual identity she occupies inside the broad range of sexual differences that inhabit those categories? A psychoanalytic critic might argue that it does, and would offer a complex reading of the text she is encountering—as does Mary Ann Doane, for example[3]—to account for the essentially sexual nature of the masochistic pleasure the woman evidently takes in her tears. I want to suggest that approaching the question from outside the psychoanalytic paradigm can lead to a different, more positive, and more potentially liberatory understanding of tears and of effeminate feeling in general. Such a reading requires careful examination of those central terms "gender" and "sex," that binary pairing whose instability has become almost legendary in the feminist theories of the 1990s, but whose strategic usefulness survives. Given the recent developments in feminist and queer theory, what do "gender" and "sex" mean now?

The question invokes a familiar conundrum of gender studies: "gender" has a relatively stable denotation—the traits or attributes a particular culture assigns as appropriate to men or to women—but "sex" has two distinct meanings. Depending on the context, "sex" refers to the genital classification of a body (as in "Sex: M or F") or means erotic encounters (as in "having sex"). Although (or perhaps because) the original distinction in gender studies between "gender" and "sex" excludes the specifically erotic denotation of "sex" from that pairing, "sexuality" has come to be almost interchangeable with "gender" in its academic usage, as if the libidinal connotations of "sex" spilled over the boundaries of the sex/gender opposition and flooded both terms. Or—if that assertion relies too heavily, for my purposes, on a psychoanalytically inspired metaphor—one could say that there is now a slippage between analyses of gender and analyses of sexuality, so that the two topics have practically collapsed into each other. This is especially evident in studies of "virtual sex," where partners often assume cross-gendered personae, entering into virtual relationships as men when their embodied identities are female, and vice versa. In this sense, studies of virtual sex have involved analyses of gender, especially since cyberspace allows individuals an unprecedented freedom to create newly gendered versions of their assumed identities.[4] However, gender is not always or exclusively expressed through sexual relations, whether "virtual" or "real"; I would argue that in contemporary U.S. culture, gender is an inescapable factor of every aspect of daily experience, both bodily and discursive. Of course this includes "having sex," but it also encompasses much more.

When gender studies began more than two decades ago, feminists quite confidently asserted a distinction between "sex," which was understood as natural, determined by biology, and "gender," which was seen as artificial, constructed by cultures. Through the late 1980s, theorists, historians, anthropologists, and cultural critics began showing ways in which "sex" is constructed, too, so that the body could no longer be taken as an unambiguous product of biology or as a sign of "real" sexual difference. After Foucault, after deconstruction, after Donna Haraway and Emily Martin and Ann Balsamo and Susan Bordo and the myriad other feminist modifiers of poststructuralist thought, the opposition between "nature" and "culture" just doesn't work anymore, no more than do the oppositions between "reality" and "artifice" or between "sex" and "gender," for that matter. Recent feminist theory enables us to see gender not so much as an entity in opposition to sex, but rather as a process, a performance, an effect of cultural patterning that always has some relationship to the subject's "sex" but never a predictable or a fixed one.[5]

This assertion depends, of course, on Judith Butler's influential idea of gender (not to mention sexuality) as "performative," but I want to emphasize that in deploying that concept, I use the term (as Butler herself does) in its specifically linguistic, rather than its theatrical, sense. As Eve Sedgwick pointed out in 1993, Butler's concept of performativity has had the effect of "placing theater and theatrical performance at front and center of questions of subjectivity and sexuality" (1); in the late 1990s, studies focusing on the body, sexuality, and gender still tended mainly to construe "performance" and "performativity" in the theatrical sense.[6] As Sedgwick resurrected the distinction between the linguistic and theatrical usages of the word to theorize a "queer performativity" at work in Henry James, I want to revisit that distinction as a way to understand how affective experience can be understood as gendered.

What precisely does Butler (1993a) mean when she writes, "Gender is not a performance that a prior subject elects to do, but gender is *performative* in the sense that it constitutes as an effect the very subject it appears to express" (314)? Jonathan Culler helpfully paraphrases the distinction made in speech-act theory by J. L. Austin between "performatives" and "constatives": "[there are] statements, or *constative* utterances, which describe a state of affairs and are true or false, and another class of utterances which are not true or false and which actually perform the action to which they refer (for example, 'I promise to pay you tomorrow' accomplishes the act of promising). These he calls *performatives*" (Culler 1982, 112). A performative speech act is an utterance that does not affirm, but constitutes its referent, such as "I bet," "I dare you," or "I now pronounce you man and wife." As Austin himself explains it, "The name ['performative'] is derived, of course, from 'perform,' the usual verb with the noun 'action': it indicates that the issuing of the utterance is the performing of an action—it is not normally thought of as just saying something" (Austin 6–7). Austin emphasizes that performatives, to be "happy" or to work, must meet certain conditions of "felicity," or else the action their utterance represents will not fully or successfully occur (14–15).

The stress in this usage of "perform," then, is on causing something to come into being, to become an actuality, not on performing a part or a role. This is the sense of the "performative" to which J. F. Lyotard refers in *The Postmodern Condition* (1984), and it is this sense—rather than the theatrical sense of "performance"—that principally informs Butler's influential essay, "Imitation and Gender Insubordination" (1993a). In theatrical usage (or in common conversation among anyone other than speech-act theorists), a "performance" is an act that is put on, a fictive identity assumed by a real person for the benefit of an audience. That sense of the word assumes an opposition between "actuality" and "performance," an opposition that mirrors the pairings of "sex" and "gender," "nature" and "culture," or, for that matter, "real feelings" and "false sentimentalism." But the linguistic usage deconstructs that opposition, for the performative utterance constitutes its own actuality: it is "neither true nor false"; nor is it, like the theatrical performance, an artifice.[7] When Butler speaks of gender as performative, she is not saying that the individual subject is "putting on an act" of gender, for that would imply that the individual subject has an "actual" gender to place in opposition to that act. As Butler puts it, "There is no 'proper' gender, a gender proper to one sex rather than another" (312); furthermore, "there is no 'I' that precedes the gender that it is said to perform" (311). If gender is performative, that means affective experiences conforming to "masculine," "feminine," or "effeminate" norms of bodily behavior don't express or mime or even imitate gender, they constitute it.

In this sense gender can be understood "as contingent and multiple— as a process rather than an *a priori* category," as Cathy Schwichtenberg (1994) puts it in "Reconceptualizing Gender: New Sites for Feminist Audience Research" (169). Schwichtenberg argues for abandoning the sexual difference model of gender (which, because of its reliance on

Lacanian constructs of identity, divides subjects into just two genders, masculine and feminine, in correspondence with two sexes). Interested in women who identify as female but are often mistaken as male, and in lesbians who reject traditional femininity in their own self-presentation, Schwichtenberg suggests that more work should be done in feminist audience research (which makes local, demonstrable claims about gender, not the broad universalizing claims of Lacanian psychoanalysis and *Screen* theory) to represent the differences among women. She suggests we need to consider the women who don't like soap opera or romance, who prefer sports, or who identify with male heroes: "To examine such disparities between gender and genre would enable us to respond to the need to more stringently problematize and pluralize the notion of gender. Indeed, the *a priori* of the 'feminine' would by necessity become less pristine and more nuanced in the process of exploring those differences between and among women, particularly women's variant forms of identification" (171).

While I acknowledge Schwichtenberg's point, I would argue that her approach can be equally useful for studying the gender performance of women who *do* "like soap opera or romance"—or what I will be calling "effeminate" persons. Thinking of femininity and its corollary, effeminacy, as processes rather than as *a priori* categories can give us a more vital and vivid picture of what gendered existence in the early 2000s is like, rather than making the tautological assumption that femininity is what feminine heterosexual women experience, whatever that might be. I will argue that effeminate affect is not the exclusive provenance of heterosexual women, or even of women per se, but that its many strengths and pleasures, including the sense of community feminist theorists have long recognized as a hallmark of "feminine" experience, are available within popular culture to women of any sexual orientation—and to gay and straight men as well.

What, after all, *does* it feel like to read a narrative, whether in print form or in film? Perhaps the question brings to mind Miller's invocation of his own body's aching back, bent over the typescript of his "Cage Aux Folles" essay, engaged in the physical act of writing that chapter of *The Novel and the Police,* or of the lawyer sitting with his feet up in the darkened theater, or the graduate student shifting uncomfortably in his chair. I am thinking more specifically, though, of the internal somatics of processing a narrative, that is, the affect or sequence of affects a narrative inspires in a reader's body. For narrative theorists up to this point, the feeling that typically comes to mind in connection with reading is directly related to sexuality: desire. As Judith Roof has argued in *Come As You Are* (1996), it is no surprise that discussions of desire and sexuality should dominate narratology, or that the combined cultures of narrative theory and gender theory would narrow their understanding of the feelings associated with reading to conform to a heterocentrically "normal" drive toward conventional closure, analogous to sexual "coming." For Roof, too, as for the theorists she critiques, narrative is always bound up with sexuality and with desire; her project suggests that the genre itself is, inevitably and unfortunately, heteronormative. I would not dispute Roof's conclusion, given the psychoanalytic paradigm in which she writes, a paradigm which has shaped much of the narrative theory and feminist theory (even what Roof calls the "structuralist" theory) written during the past two decades. I want to suggest, though, that stepping *outside* the psychoanalytic paradigm to think about gender and reading can open up our understanding of gendered bodily experience beyond the realm of the specifically sexual, and can make available for analysis other readerly feelings than just "desire."

But—keeping in mind my Preface's opening vignette about the facial expressions the young woman experiences when her Dickens novel gives her a surprise—when I ask what reading feels like, I mean something more than slouching in an armchair, or lying in the sun, or killing time on a bus, or running on a Stairmaster holding a book. I mean the physical impact of narratives themselves: the constriction in the throat and the dampness of the eye that signal the sentimental response, or the acceleration of the pulse that comes with excitement or apprehension, or the agitation of the chest and diaphragm that constitute a laugh, or the tension that accompanies suspense, or that arching in the back of the throat that heralds the yawn of boredom. Narratives mark readers' bodies with these effects, and if the cry, the laugh, the gasp, the yawn is only ephemeral in any given instance, certain genres invoke these physical responses in predictable, formulaic patterns. A sentimental novel, a "women's weepy" film, a narrative structured by the marriage plot, a serialized fiction all follow established conventions for inspiring certain feelings at particular junctures of the story. Such popular narrative forms are what I call technologies of affect, providing structures of feeling in the daily lives of their devotees. Significantly, these genres are also strongly gendered: sentimental films and novels, soap operas, and marriage-plot narratives have long been associated with effeminate audiences, while certain forms of historical and science-fiction serial narrative have audiences I would have to call "not-effeminate," for lack of an existing antonym.

When I say that each of these genres is a technology for writing gender on and through our bodies, I am thinking of the enculturated body quite literally as a text in progress. In *Volatile Bodies: Toward a Corporeal*

Feminism (1994), Elizabeth Grosz points out how postmodern philosophical traditions elaborate a metaphor of the body as "a page or strip on
which a social text . . . is written": "The tools of body engraving—social,
surgical, epistemic, disciplinary—all mark, indeed constitute, bodies in
culturally specific ways; the writing instruments—pen, stylus, spur, laser
beam, clothing, diet, exercise—function to incise the body's blank page"
(117).[8] If we think of culture the way post-Marxist and post-Foucauldian
cultural studies have taught us to do, not as a product but a process, we
can see the instruments Grosz identifies as examples of cultural technologies. For instance, the stylus of the tattoo artist, the laser beam of the cosmetic surgeon, the diet of Lean Cuisine and Slim-Fast or of four-course
dinners, the roller-blading and the iron-pumping are not just metaphors
signifying "writing on the body," but are the means through which cultural practices quite literally mark and shape the contemporary bourgeois
body. I am arguing that we should think of narrative structures as another of these instruments, as devices that work through readers' bodily feelings to produce and reproduce the physical fact of bourgeois subjectivity.

Grosz's comparison of the body to a "page or strip" suggests a surface
that can be written upon, then turned over to reveal the next page, or the
next panel of the cartoon. The linear temporality of this figure corre-
sponds to received notions of narrative, commonly understood as a literary structure with a beginning, a middle, and an end, unfolding over
time. Sentimental and serial fictions, like all narratives, do follow a linear
temporality, but I am suggesting that their physical effects mark readers'
bodies in a more three-dimensional way than the image of a page implies.
Intensely conscious of the negative connotations such a metaphor will
bring up, I visualize the body not as flattened-out paper, but as rounded
and supple plastic. Perhaps the connotations can be ameliorated by an
allusion to "the plastic arts." As devotees of popular-cultural genres repeat
their reading performances, they reengrave the genre's affective patterns
on their bodies while reexperiencing its conventional narrative moves.
Written over and over again with the genre's somatic effects, the reader's
body is subject to patterns of feelings that carry strong connotations of
gender and of class. Figuratively speaking, those patterns mold the body's
plasticity, leaving the marks and the shapes characteristic of the feelings
their genres typically bring up. By identifying narrative patterns and
strategies structuring each of these popular cultural forms, this book
uncovers the textual machinery inside these narrative technologies of gender, and seeks to reveal—from the inside out—the structures of feeling
that constitute contemporary gendered experience.

Effeminacy: A Third Term for Gender Studies

Because I am loathe to reify gendered patterns of behavior in British and U.S. mainstream culture as somehow eternally or essentially "masculine" or "feminine," I am introducing into that typical pairing a third term that has also emerged as part of the vocabulary of sexuality studies in the past decade: "effeminacy." While the important role "effeminacy" plays as a category of analysis in sexuality studies cannot be put aside, I am interested in new possibilities it presents for use in discussing gender.[9] What makes "effeminacy" especially intriguing is the fact that, unlike the words marking the other matrices employed in feminist theory such as "man/woman," "masculine/feminine," or "male/female," it has no opposite, unless it be a neologistic construction, something like "the not-effeminate" or "effeminacy—NOT." To underline this unusual feature of the notion of the effeminate, I will, in the course of my analysis, place it at one end of a spectrum separating its most extreme manifestations from what I will call "the antieffeminate."

As it does not fit comfortably into a binary opposition (that is, because its opposite must be coined for the purpose of making distinctions or mapping a spectrum of the more-or-less effeminate characteristics and feelings I will be discussing), "effeminacy" interestingly complicates the symmetry of the binarisms underpinning contemporary gender theory. The opposite of "effeminacy," according to the dictionary, is "manliness." This denotative oddity points to the asymmetry in dominant culture's attitudes toward gendered behavior. If "male" is supposed to be the opposite of "female," "man" the opposite of "woman," and "masculine" the opposite of "feminine" (as suggested by the structuralist model of sex and gender on which poststructuralist analyses are based), then would not "womanliness" logically be the opposite of "manliness"? But womanliness is not used as an antonym to manliness, nor does womanliness mean the same thing as effeminacy, the acknowledged opposite of manliness. Womanliness denotes the traits "becoming to a woman," which would make it a synonym for femininity; manliness denotes the traits "befitting a man," also called "masculinity." Effeminacy, though, denotes both "qualities more often associated with women than men" and "weakness and excessive refinement." Indeed, women are seldom called effeminate, probably because the culture still takes it for granted that women are already automatically characterized by "weakness and excessive refinement," particularly in the realms of feeling.

Men whose gender performance includes details coded as feminine— men who for instance roll their eyes, speak with implicit italics and exclamation points, and allow themselves to cry—are called "effeminate," just as men wearing panty hose or lipstick or men who move with what used to be called a "mincing" walk would be. Implicit in the label of "effeminacy" is the sexual position "more often associated with women than men," the sexual role of the one who is penetrated—hence the widespread association in Western culture, recently traced by literary historians back through modern European literature, of "effeminacy" with male homosexuality.[10] And yet, for every sexual partner (gay or straight, male or female) who is penetrated there must also be (at least) one who penetrates; "effeminacy" does not begin to cover the range of gender performance to be found among gay men, let alone women. The man in my Preface watching *Saving Private Ryan* conceals and denies his tears, to avoid signaling the effeminacy those tears connote; the man who pouts and rolls his eyes while watching *As the World Turns* is already engaged in an act associated with "weakness and excessive refinement" (the habitual watching of soap operas), even before his reactions register as feelings with gendered connotations. If the first man is straight and the second man gay, that can perhaps help account for their respective degrees of willingness to exhibit "effeminate" displays of feeling. I would argue, though, that the bare fact of their crying or rolling their eyes over their chosen texts tells us nothing about their sexual identities. Both are engaging in moments of effeminate feeling. And why—I ask, as a "feminine" woman prone to displays of "weakness and excessive refinement," if that is what we want to call crying over movies and books—is that something to be embarrassed about? From what position of objectivity and appropriateness are we to judge feelings as "weak"? When does "refinement" phase into "excess"? I am interested in rehabilitating "effeminacy" from the pejorative status it currently holds, to mount a defense of "effeminate feeling" in the name of antiessentialist feminism.

Effeminacy, then, is performative; feelings, too, can be understood as performative: to say this is to understand the body not as the location where gender and affect are expressed, but rather as the medium through which they come into being. As Teresa de Lauretis and others have argued, culture is filled with, even predicated upon technologies of gender, forms and structures that work to perpetuate gender difference between women and men. The principal goal of this study is to analyze some of those popular cultural forms that have operated in the Victorian and postmodern periods on a daily basis within individual subjects' lives, prompting feelings that carry gendered connotations, constituting the experience of gender itself.

Feelings: How Do You *Really* Feel ?

The refrain of a popular song from 1991 haunts me: in "Walking in Memphis," Marc Cohn sings, "But do I really feel the way I feel?" When I notice that this song is stuck in my mind, I ask myself, what would it mean to "*really* feel the way I feel"? Does the question imply that it is possible to feel a way that I *don't* "really" feel? Or, indeed, that I have "real" feelings which I am not feeling? Perhaps I have been taught to think skeptically of such lyrics by Judith Butler's (1993) artful deconstruction of Aretha Franklin's "You Make Me Feel (Like a Natural Woman)": "Although Aretha appears to be all too glad to have her naturalness confirmed, she also seems fully and paradoxically mindful that that confirmation is never guaranteed, that the effect of naturalness is only achieved as a consequence of that moment of heterosexual recognition" (317). Just as Aretha's assertion undercuts the naturalness of her feeling natural, the question "Do I really feel the way I feel?" casts doubt upon its own premises. If it is possible that the answer is no, then can there be such a thing as "real feelings"? And, even if they could exist, if we can't know them by feeling them, how could we possibly know whether or not they are "real"?

Yet I don't think of Cohn's question as nonsense—far from it. The question "Do I really feel the way I feel?" is perfectly intelligible in the context of modern popular- and high-culture models of emotional experience. As I will argue, one of the legacies of modernism has been the belief that individual subjects are repositories of "real" feelings, and that sincere and authentic emotional experience can be distinguished from false sentimentalism and affectation. This is the legacy of "self psychology," prevalent in the self-help movement and related though not identical to the "ego psychology" elaborated within psychoanalysis. Psychoanalysis—with its complex diagnostic system for translating perceived affect into unconscious drives and motives—was continually popularized (one could say "trivialized") during the later twentieth century into simplistic generalizations about repression and sublimation that suggest the average neurotic person is hopelessly out of touch with "real" feelings. A popular Los Angeles radio psychologist writes in a self-help manual from the 1970s: "If you don't live in your feelings, you don't live in the real world. Feelings are the truth. What you do with them will decide whether you live in honesty or by a lie" (Viscott 22); he elaborates: "By learning to allow feelings to flow naturally, the world each of us perceives can also change and become more real, and we can become more accurate, more *honest,* in the way we feel about it" (32). According to this reasoning, each of us possesses real feelings, but if we have not taken the proper psychological precautions, the "road less traveled" as a pop-psych manual of the 1980s called it, we may not really feel the way we feel.

Emotional life in the mainstream United States at the century's turn raises questions about the reality of feelings in ways that could hardly have been imagined twenty or even ten years ago. The "cosmetic" use of anti-depressants and other legalized mood-altering drugs, for instance, raises questions about the extent to which feelings emanate from personality or from chemistry, and about how the latter can have transformative effects upon the former. If persons who are not clinically depressed take Prozac because it makes them feel "better than well,"[11] do they really feel the way they feel? The growing popularity of Twelve-Step programs for recovery from chemical dependency, codependency, overeating, gambling, and sex-and-love addiction is another example of a cultural technology for struc-turing participants' affective lives. No one entering a program of recovery "really feels like" giving up the addiction or dependency that brought him or her there; such a feeling would obviate the necessity for participating in a program. "Take the actions," advises Alcoholics Anonymous in one of its most potent slogans, "and the feelings will follow." Impressed though he or she might be at how effective this approach is for those who are willing to go through the motions outlined in the twelve steps, the recovering person may well ask whether the feelings that follow are "real-ly felt." And what about feelings in cyberspace? Communications schol-ars and science-fiction writers alike are asking, for instance, in what sense cybersexual relationships are really relationships. If feelings are induced and expressed in a virtual medium, are the feelings themselves only virtu-al or are they really real? None of these questions can be simply or straightforwardly answered. We can approach them, though, in the con-text of a postmodern understanding of the self not as an ineluctable essence, but as a constructed entity. "Do I really feel the way I feel?" is not a stupid question, but it is not an answerable question, either; it opens a window on to a *mise-en-abyme,* a complex set of assumptions, reflections, and contradictions that lead to no clear end point, no image of what a "real" feeling would ultimately be.

What is the range of feelings one might really feel? Depending on your perspective, the range may be alarmingly narrow or overwhelmingly wide. According to Twelve-Step aphorisms, there are only four basic feelings: "mad, glad, sad, and scared"; everything else is just an attitude, or how you think about the emotions you are experiencing (for example, "resentment" is anger that has been nursed with obsessive thinking; "despair" is sadness that lacks perspective). Although this idea is not to be found in any of the official literature of Alcoholics Anonymous, its prevalence in some Twelve-Step meetings suggests the influence of cognitive psychology (via the written and televised teachings of such practitioners as John Bradshaw, as well as the psychotherapeutic experiences of some Twelve-Step program members), which holds that basic emotional impulses are experienced first as undifferentiated affect, then translated through thought into identifiable emotions. At the other extreme, where feelings might be enumerated and differentiated in their full spectrum of variety, the Library of Congress classificatory system suggests there are no fewer than fifty-four of them, helpfully arranged under the heading of "Emotion" in alphabetical order. To give only a selection: they run from Ambivalence, Anger, Anxiety, and Awe; through Cheerfulness, Crying, Defeat, Desire, Despair, Disappointment, and Discontent; on to Happiness, Hate, Helplessness, Homesickness, Hope, and Horror; through Regret, Rejection, Remorse, Resentment, Sadness, Self-confidence, Shame, Smiling, Surprise, Sympathy, Tenderness, and Timidity; to end, appropriately enough, on Wonder and Worry. I find the catalogue's valiant and comprehensive attempt to impose any kind of order on such a tangle of emotional conditions (even if that order is only alphabetical) both amusing and poignant, for the list is of course as inadequate as it is ambitious. Looking over the shelves of a research library's collection on the subject of emotion may evoke a similarly rueful reaction. Some emotions are the topics of many books (Anger, Anxiety, Love, and Stress each filled several shelves at an up-to-date university library in the 1990s). Others seem left out altogether: where in this classificatory system would "ruefulness" be placed? Perhaps that doesn't qualify as an emotion, but would more properly be considered an attitude, or maybe a conglomeration of the more primary emotions of—in alphabetical order, of course—Ambivalence, Disappointment, Empathy, Frustration, Helplessness, Laughter, and Sympathy. Other feelings associated with the act of reading are also absent from the Library of Congress list: where is suspense? or absorption? or boredom? If the history of the world's literature, of poetry and fiction from every culture, tells us little else with certainty and consistency, it communicates what everybody of course already knows: emotion is elusive and complex, ineffable, inexpressible, and ultimately impossible fully to communicate or indeed to analyze. While I will draw sometimes on the lexicon of emotion, my focus will be upon something rather less ambitious in this study of the physical experience of reading: that is, the somatic, bodily aspect of a selection of reactions—crying, hope and worry, interest and boredom, suspense and relief—that reading can invoke. My topic is not the generation, motivation, and anatomy of emotion in the individual self—the proper subject, as I take it, of the psychology of emotion—but rather the patterns of textual cues for invoking these bodily experiences in the popular-cultural forms I have mentioned.

Psychologists working on emotion currently use the term *feelings* to refer to the subjective experience of the physical aspects of emotions.[12] "Feelings" are often distinguished from "emotions" as being less complex, more purely physical, less motivated, and less motivating to action.[13] "Affect" is a synonym for "feelings" in the social-psychological and philosophical terminology adopted by scholars who have tried to narrow down that Library of Congress list of fifty-four possibilities for empirical study. For Silvan Tomkins, for example, there are "nine innate affects," three of them positive (interest or excitement, enjoyment or joy, and surprise or startle) and six of them negative (distress or anguish, fear or terror, shame or humiliation, contempt, disgust, and anger or rage) (Tomkins, in Scherer et al., 167–68). Each of the nine has a characteristic facial expression associated with it, an expression by which interlocutors might interpret one's feelings, to be sure, but which does not primarily serve a communicative function. For Tomkins and others, like him, working in the psychoevolutionary and psychophysiological traditions, the facial affect—the feeling experienced through and transmitted by the skin and the muscles of the person who smiles with enjoyment or cries with distress—constitutes the emotion. Colleagues and competitors of Tomkins's posit six basic affects (Ekman), or eight (Plutchik), or ten (Izard), but for my purposes, the exact number is not really important. What is important is these researchers' suggestion that affect is not primarily a direct or indirect reflection or expression of an interior emotional state. On the contrary, they have argued by different means and to various ends that the physical experience of feelings can be understood as itself the constituent fact of emotional life.

Depending on the researcher's perspective, then, feelings may be understood as the outward or mental expression of interior emotion—as in the models favored by cognitive and psychoanalytic approaches—or as themselves the constituents of emotion, as researchers working in psychophysiological traditions would say. Literary criticism and film theory, shaped as they have always been by psychoanalytic approaches, have tended to favor the first of these models, the concept of feelings as expressive. By doing so, these scholarly traditions have granted privilege to the idea that every person harbors "real" feelings, whether consciously or subconsciously experienced, and that literary texts tap into those feelings in more or less legitimate ways.[14] In what follows, I will be arguing that modernist aesthetics also favored this expressive model, and that a concept of feelings as the outward signs of internal emotional states helped to shape the high modernist prejudice against popular cultural forms and their audiences.[15]

The alternative model—the idea that feelings are not so much expressive as they are performative, bringing into being the emotional states they betoken—has its roots in the nineteenth-century psychophilosophical tradition of philosophers and physiologists such as William James, Carl Lange, and François Delsarte. As James put it in 1884: "The more closely I scrutinize my states, the more persuaded I become that whatever moods, affections, and passions I have, are in very truth constituted by, and made up of, those bodily changes we ordinarily call their expression or consequence; and the more it seems to me that if I were to become corporeally anesthetic, I should be excluded from the life of the affections, harsh and tender alike, and drag out an existence of merely cognitive or intellectual form" (quoted in Cornelius 1996, 61). Lange, a Danish physiologist writing just a year later, puts a related idea a different way: "Take away the bodily symptoms from a frightened individual; let his pulse beat calmly, his look be firm, his color normal, his movements quick and sure, his speech strong and his thoughts clear; and what remains of his fear?" (quoted in Cornelius 1996, 66). To be sure, such an approach grants nothing to the unconscious, and would prove unsatisfactory for an examination of all the subtleties and complexities of emotional life. But as a way of thinking about feelings, the somatic manifestations of emotion, this approach is, I think, peculiarly suited to the project of understanding feelings in both Victorian and postmodern popular culture. Given that this Victorian-era concept of feelings has recently been revived in the work of Tomkins and his colleagues, this performative model is perhaps more appropriate than modernism's assumptions are to the discussion of both Victorian and contemporary popular texts and their effects upon their reading audiences. To think of feelings as "performative" is not, within this framework, to think of them as less than "real." It is rather to put both a Victorian and a postmodernist spin on ideas of what "real feelings" might be and of where they come from. It is also to take a radical departure from the assumptions we inherit from Aristotle and from Freud.

Aristotle's *Poetics* takes for granted certain theories about how emotions operate in the body, theories which persist—as we will see in chapter 2—in literary criticism as they do in neo-Freudian psychoanalysis. Quite casually, Aristotle explains in part 6 of the *Poetics* that one of tragedy's defining features is that it will "through pity and fear [effect] the proper purgation of these emotions" (27). This theory of "catharsis" has been taken in the twentieth century to mean that audience members' bodies or psyches contain a given quantity of pity and of fear, and that the experience of weeping at a tragedy constitutes the "proper purgation," the healthy and controlled venting or draining of those emotions. According to Aristotle's more detailed description of the effect in part 13, "Pity is aroused by unmerited misfortunes, fear by the misfortune of a man like ourselves" (33). In other words, the "fear" effect relies on the audience's identification with the tragic hero and the "pity" effect depends on the ethical and moral conclusions the audience draws from the hero's fate. Both these effects are, then, strictly culture-bound: they cannot be assumed to work upon audiences who—for whatever reasons having to do with ethnicity, nationality, sexuality, class, gender, or era—do not identify with the hero or who do not see his fate as unmerited. In any given tragedy, then, the effects themselves are not essential or eternal, but dependent upon the psychological and moral orientation of the actual audience. Aristotle's expected effects are historically situated and so is his model of emotional experience. "Catharsis" is a theory of response, not a natural fact about human emotion: it is a powerful and persistent theory, but it is only one among many possible ways to think about what is happening when readers cry over texts.

The pervasiveness of the catharsis model in modern literary critical practice can be traced as much to Freud as to Aristotle. Based as it is on a "container metaphor" for emotion, in which the mind or body is figured as a repository of a fluid standing in for emotion, catharsis typifies Freud's way of thinking about emotional process. Zoltán Kövecses (1990) has demonstrated the pervasiveness in language of the container metaphor for emotion, showing that in everyday discourse, emotions are figured as fluids in a container (as in "she was filled with emotion," "emotion welled up inside her," "he managed to bottle up his emotions," "I could barely keep it in anymore" [146, 150]) which share certain natural properties with other liquids (e.g., "As the emotion gets more intense, the fluid goes out of the container: He poured out his feelings to her. She overflowed with emotion" [147]); "When the emotion gets too intense, the container explodes: There was an outburst of passion. All her pent up feelings burst out" (150); and "Emotion can be let out under control: He let out his emotions slowly. The teacher vented all her passions at us" (150). Commonplace as these container metaphors for emotion are, Kövecses nevertheless argues that "the theory that has been the most influential of the views that build on the container metaphor in large measure is Freud's" (156). Freud's discussion of catharsis would be one of the sources of that influence.

In their classic explanation of the mechanics of hysteria, Breuer and Freud (1957) posit that a traumatic memory can only healthily fade if "there has been an energetic reaction to the event that provokes an affect," reactions being "the whole class of voluntary and involuntary reflexes—from tears to acts of revenge—in which, as experience shows us, the affects are discharged" (8). The reaction to the trauma is "cathartic" if it is "adequate," but "if the reaction is suppressed, the affect remains attached to the memory" (8). If, however, "there is no such reaction, whether in deeds or words, or in the mildest cases in tears, any recollection of the event retains its affective tone" (8). In other words, unless the emotion is purged or discharged, it remains dammed up in the body, and until the proper catharsis occurs, it will continue—through hysterical manifestations—to affect the body's functions. As Carol Tavris (1982) summarizes this view, "Freud imagined that the libido was a finite amount of energy that powers our internal battles. If the energy is blocked here, it must find release there" (37).

As Tavris is quick to point out, however, and as Kövecses's linguistic approach to the question emphasizes, Freud's language of energy and catharsis is metaphoric, and having never been "scientifically proven," remains a way of talking about how emotions function, rather than a definitive account of that process. Critiquing psychotherapeutic practices which take literally the idea that "emotional energy is a fixed quantity that can be dammed up or, conversely, that can 'flood' the system" (22), Tavris calls this "ventilationist" view into question. According to recent work on the expression of hostile feelings, the "reaction" through "affect" associated with anger may not function cathartically in all cases, but may sometimes only rehearse the affect. Since, as Tavris points out, "any emotional arousal will eventually simmer down, if you just wait long enough" (122), people who vent hostile feelings will eventually feel better, as will people who do not vent them. But the people who act upon their feelings will "be acquiring a cathartic habit" (126). To shout or hit someone, she explains, is not necessarily a vent for anger—it can instead be seen as a reinforcement of shouting or hitting behavior. If this is true, then perhaps to cry is not necessarily a purgation of fear and pity—or of whatever emotion inspired the tears.

I am not presuming to say that Freud's model is not "right." Rather, I am bringing forward the fact that such models are "historicizable," that they have their respective places in cultural history and, doubtless, their influences upon discourse about emotions and art. This observation opens the possibility that other accounts of the body's relation to emotion might alter our view of the role texts play in stirring up feelings, or more precisely, might put us in the position of grasping how an era's notions on the matter might color its audiences' tastes. Aristotle and the twentieth-century critics who do not question his assumptions say that tragedy is cathartic and therefore good. I am suggesting that sentimentalism is pointedly *not* cathartic, that it does not vent or drain emotions, but that it rather encourages readers to rehearse and reinforce the feelings it evokes. Does that make sentimentalism bad? Within an Aristotelian framework, perhaps, but not from the perspective of Freud's predecessors, whose notions of psychophysiology differ markedly from the model I have been describing.

The modernist idea that the emotions fill the container of the body requires conceptualizing a binary split between body and mind. Joseph Roach, whose work on the history of theatrical performance raises this issue (1985), points out that this mind/body split was not current in nineteenth-century psychology and physiology. The dominant idea of the dynamics of mind and body during the Victorian period in Europe and America was a version of monism, elaborated by George Henry Lewes (1892) in his capacity as naturalist (and applied in his capacity as literary critic).[16] Monism sees the mind and body not as a duality, but as a continuum, and in this respect can be understood as a precedent for later twentieth-century feminist challenges to the mind/body binarism.[17] Lewes organized his continuum into four levels. First is the level of "neural tremors," the sensory data received by the body; second, the level of sensation (made up of groupings of tremors); third, the level of image (made up of groupings of sensations); and fourth, the level of symbol or idea. The four levels can act interchangeably as stimuli, one upon another: for example, the idea can evoke the sensation, or the neural tremor can evoke the image. As Roach explains, Lewes's model informs William James's conviction that "the physiological manifestation of the emotion *is* the emotion . . . it is because we weep that we feel sad, it is because we . . . tremble that we feel afraid" (192). As I have suggested above, this idea—that the physical signs of emotion are not expressions or reflections of an interior state, but are the constitutive elements of the emotion itself—closely resembles the postmodern theory of performativity. To cry is not to express an internal feeling: to cry is to feel, for William James as for Butler or Sedgwick.

Thinking in terms of performance is one good way to illustrate the differences between the modernist/Freudian container metaphor for emotion, and the Victorian/Jamesian psychophysiological model. Consider the differences between the Victorian and modern periods' dominant ideas about theatrical acting. "According to the principles laid down by both François Delsarte and William James," reports Martha Banta (1987), "physical acts initiate emotions and make them authentic. When your body assumes a pose in a particular setting, that pose becomes your sign. As you stand, so you feel and are" (647).[18] The Delsarte to whom Banta refers was a French philosopher (1811–1871) whose disciples codified his theories of pose and gesture, adapting them into conventions to be used by melodramatic actors and artists' models. Those conventions were entirely opposed to popular modern notions about how actors employ the relation between the body and the emotions. A twentieth-century "method actor," following the precepts of Stanislavski, would attempt to "get into character" before performing a part. This entails the actor's concentrating on "becoming" the character internally, in order to represent him or her bodily on stage or before the camera. In the practice of such method actors as Marlon Brando, Dustin Hoffman, or Robert DeNiro, becoming a character means drawing upon memory of lived experience to recreate emotions the actor has felt in circumstances comparable to those being represented in the diegesis. In other words, the method actor draws upon that reservoir of stored emotion to vent it during the performance. In this modernist style of acting, the gesture—be it a subtly raised eyebrow or a dramatically brandished arm—serves to express the feeling which the actor who is "in character" is "really" experiencing.

Delsarte's nineteenth-century idea of acting stands this concept on its head: Instead of seeing gestures and poses as expressions of real interior states, he saw them as vehicles for producing those states. In Delsarte's scheme, each body part (the hand, the torso, the forearm, etc.) is connected to *L'Esprit, L'Ame,* or *La Vie,* categories his followers translated as "the Mental, the Moral, and the Vital." In a more elaborate version of the kind of continuum Lewes had envisioned among body, mind, and feeling, the mental zones of the body are linked to the operations of the intellect, the moral zones are linked to emotions, and the vital zones are linked to sensation. The chest, for example, is a mental zone (the Delsarteans do not explain why), and the sob (a kind of breathing that puts the chest into a violent or "hysteric" motion) is—according to one of Delsarte's adapters—a bodily motion that actors must use "very carefully," because it both signifies and produces "a mind unbalanced" (Stebbins 1977, 288). For Delsarte, then, the gesture not only expresses the emotion and the state of mind, it brings them into being. Hence the actress positioned with face upturned, right hand raised to the forehead, left hand clenched and arm extended behind her, eyes closed and brows in an inverted *v,* will not just reflect or portray the sentiment her pose represents in a Delsartean handbook ("Mine woes afflict this spirit sore" [Banta 1987, 645]), she will *feel* it. The feeling will be "realized"; the pose will bring the affect into the actress's emotional experience of the moment, and her body's bringing the feeling into physical presence will transmit its effect to the audience.

Delsarte's formulation, of course, reverses the container metaphor on which the principle of catharsis is based. The modern view says we weep because we feel sad, and in weeping we get that sadness "out of our systems." Based on essentialist assumptions about "human nature," the modern view leads to the evaluation of some feelings as more genuine, more fully human than others—which leads inexorably to the denigration of the emotional experience of persons whose cultural or social marginality marks their feelings as "different." Perhaps the most unexpected aspect of the Victorian view is the easy alliance it forms with postmodernism, in that both reject essentialism as a way of accounting for interior experience. Furthermore, the Victorian idea that we feel sad *because* we weep puts a radically different spin on weeping's ultimate effect. This means that from the Victorian perspective, crying over *Uncle Tom's Cabin* or *Little Women* did not drain a reservoir of stored feelings, nor did it debilitate readers from taking action in the extratextual world. Instead, crying was seen as creating and promoting the feelings, which then might presumably serve as goads to acting, or indeed to being, in the "real world." Newspaper movie reviewers' assumptions about the cathartic effects of "women's weepies" notwithstanding, a twenty-first-century take on the experience of the crying effeminate audience might more closely resemble this Victorian model of spectatorship than the Freudian/psychoanalytic model that has dominated theoretical discussions of audience response.

If nineteenth-century sentimental novelists and Hollywood film producers are not consciously aware of such theories of the relations among bodily action and emotion, they seem at least to have been operating under assumptions similar to those that inspire the theories. The sentimental novelist, like the Delsartean actor, relies on a set of "mechanical" exercises (as Delsarte's detractors called his gymnastic drill for actors, and indeed as high-culture commentators call the "manipulative" techniques of tear-jerking films). The Delsartean actor is using those postures to bring into being a real feeling; the sentimental novelist is using technologies of affect to get the body of the reader into the pose that would generate real compassion or real joy, the pose of weeping. The narrator of the nineteenth-century sentimental novel puts the reader through the drill, using techniques established in such late eighteenth-century precursors as Susanna Rowson's *Charlotte Temple* (1791). Although a critic as historically minded as Cathy Davidson (1989) suggests that Rowson's novel worked on its audiences' emotions through their identification with its heroine (170), I think that identification (another post-Freudian model

frequently imposed on the presumed reading experience of earlier generations) may not have been the only process at work in Rowson's crying
readers.[19] Many of the "mechanical" techniques still operating in today's
"good-cry" texts must have been at least partly responsible for that first
U.S. best-seller's emotional impact.

Literary critical and cultural studies work on audiences' affective
response has developed, up to this point, in two distinct traditions: the
humanities-based tradition of Freudian and Lacanian psychoanalytic criticism and the social sciences–based field of behavioristic "effects"
research. Within the humanities, film theory in particular and narrative
theory more broadly have generally adopted a psychoanalytic understanding of the emotions that motivate readers' activities. As I mentioned at the
outset, work on reading and feelings has mainly centered on one emotion
that is not one of Tomkins's basic affects but that dominates Freud's and
Lacan's account of emotional experience: desire. In psychoanalytic criticism[20] and film theory (particularly *Screen* theory), desire is almost always
construed in terms of libidinal impulses, commonly understood as sexuality. Under the rubric of psychoanalysis, all feelings are in some sense sexual (whether they are repressions, sublimations, transferences, cathexes, or
fetishizations, to list only a few of the ways that sexual feelings get translated or communicated within psychoanalytic thought). The end point of
most psychoanalytic projects considering gender and reader response is a
discussion of sexuality understood in specifically libidinal terms.[21] In the
section on "Effeminacy," above, I have outlined some of the drawbacks of
conflating gender and sexuality, as psychoanalytic approaches tend to do,
in the context of contemporary feminist theory. This book is an experiment in what might happen to literary and cultural criticism if we try to
analyze affect outside the psychoanalytic paradigm. I concur with Eve
Sedgwick and Adam Frank's (1995) suggestion that Tomkins's psychology—or, in this case, the psychological and philosophical traditions within which he is working—might be "a different place to begin" (7).

To be sure, psychoanalysis has not been the only place for media studies to begin, for the social sciences tradition of "effects" research has
approached the question of audiences' feelings from a radically antipsy-
choanalytic, bodily based perspective. Researchers working in mass communications and social psychology have developed a substantial amount
of work on "media effects" that seeks objectively to demonstrate how people feel about films and television programs they are watching. Their
methodologies range from administering surveys to soap-opera viewers, to
wiring up college students with electrodes and noting their physiological
reactions when exposed to various genres of emotionally incendiary texts.

From an antiessentialist, poststructuralist perspective, such positivistic projects are almost too easy to critique. The psychophysiological approach to studying affect presents a challenge to behaviorism that is, perhaps, less predictable than the form such a critique would take. According to Sedgwick and Frank, "Against the behaviorists, Tomkins consistently argues that relevant stimulus for the affect system includes internal as well as external events, concluding firmly that there is no basis—and certainly not the basis of internal versus external—for a definitional distinction between response and stimulus" (11). They illustrate this observation with an amusing account of Tomkins's work on the variety of reactions subjects express to the stimulus of electric shock, which range—counterintuitively enough—from "Feels like when Papa spanked" to "It's maddening" to "I'm not getting much out of this—I hope you are" to "I like the shocks" to "Feels like a sport with a bet on" to "Oh, Lord, I'm falling asleep" (11). If a stimulus as specific as an electric shock cannot be counted upon to produce any one particular affective response, then what can be the objective, predictive value of information gathered through media-effects research on subjects engaged in responding to complex filmic texts? The variables of internal and external factors—the subjects' mood, personality, memories, experiences, associations, physical condition, and so on—are so numerous as to break down the distinction, as Sedgwick and Frank assert, between internal and external, between stimulus and response.

While I capitalize on media-effects researchers' findings whenever I can, this book makes no claims to the level of scientificity their projects achieve. The feelings I am interested in mapping are subjectively experienced and self-reported; while I try to draw from a variety of sources (Internet discussion groups, published accounts of reading habits, and conversations) so as not to be limited merely to discussing my own reading experiences, there is nothing objective about my approach. I do not offer a repeatable or predictive experiment to determine readers' responses; I make no generalizable claims about what reading feels like for everyone or even for any particular reading subject in all circumstances and at all times. While I doubt that readers are usually conscious of the cultural effects I am trying to identify, the feelings that interest me are not subconscious or subliminal, but vividly present in the physical experience of persons encountering texts. Such feelings are "real" in the sense that readers experience them as somatic, that is to say bodily, events. They are not, however, either verifiable or quantifiable. Hence, my analysis focuses not on the "real" feelings of (all) "real" readers, but on generic textual patterns that structure the feelings of fans of specific popular genres.[22]

What seems most promising about the psychophysiological approach to the study of affect is its potential for liberating individual subjects from the notion of a "core self," a self that can only be identified, diagnosed, and evaluated by a hegemonic authority that has the power to see, know, and name the "other." No one has access to anyone's "core self" except those—like the psychoanalyst, the radio psychologist, the humanist literary critic—who assert their own authority by claiming to see and to name it in somebody else. Sedgwick and Frank point to Tomkins's usefulness in this respect: "Sublimely alien, we found [Tomkins's] psychology, to the developmental presumption or prescription of a core self; sublimely *resistant,* we might have added, to such presumption—except that the sublimity lies in an exemplary cartographic distance, not in a dialectical struggle" (7). In the chapters that follow, I will explore what can happen to cultural studies if we try proceeding at Tomkins's "cartographic distance" from prevailing assumptions about reading and feelings. Eschewing the idea of a "core self," I will argue against thinking of "real" feelings as "authentic," "sincere," or "honest," because I believe that such approaches to affective experience have served under patriarchy seriously to disadvantage effeminate persons—and I mean to include some gay and heterosexual men and bi- and transsexuals, as well as some women in this category—by devaluing their everyday experiences of emotional life. Who is to judge whether the woman sobbing at a melodramatic movie is experiencing a "sincere," "authentic," "real" emotion, or whether she is "merely" being "manipulated" by sentimentalism? She is having a good cry, experiencing a feeling, and the tears in her eyes and convulsive actions of her chest are real enough to qualify as manifestations of an affect. As I and others have argued before, it is not a coincidence that at the same time this culture condemns her body's activity, her feeling, as "inauthentic," or as a betrayal of her "core self," it also condemns her (gendered) tears as effeminate.

Forms: Feminist Narratology and Close Reading

Each chapter of this book is devoted to a form that has worked during the past century and a half as a technology of gender, inscribing masculine or feminine affective experience on readers' bodies. By "forms" I mean genres of narrative fiction, more or less formulaically working through conventional patterns of story and discourse. My forms include sentimental narrative, sometimes called the "women's weepy," in both the nineteenth and twentieth centuries; the marriage-plot narrative, in nineteenth-century novels and contemporary films that either follow or disrupt the girl-meets/loses/gets-boy scenario; and serialized narrative, as it is played out in Victorian and contemporary serial novels addressed to not-effeminate audiences and in daytime television soap operas addressed to frankly effeminate viewers. I use the term *narrative* inclusively, to refer to elements of both "story" (or what a narrative represents as happening) and "discourse" (or how the story gets transmitted through narrative devices).[23] My method singles out particular aspects of each of these forms—for instance, the rhetorical devices and intertextual references that combine to evoke the "good cry," or the instances of repetition and recapitulation that typify serial form—to consider their affective impact upon readers who are conversant with and susceptible to particular popular genres. I am arguing that we should think of narrative structures as devices that work through readers' bodily feelings to produce and reproduce the physical fact of gendered subjectivity. While postmodern philosophy and cultural studies have gone a long way in the last decade toward sketching out the parameters of how culture works upon the body, I think narrative theory—and specifically, I mean feminist narratology—can give us the tools to get much more concrete about how that process operates. The tools I have in mind are two that have sometimes conflicted with each other in the elaboration of narrative theory, namely "poetics," or the systematic description of narrative systems, and "close reading." Fifteen years ago, I was arguing that narratology could offer feminist criticism a method for demonstrating its broad claims about gender difference; today I would make a similar case for the usefulness of *feminist* narratology to cultural studies.

What "narratology" suggested to feminist critics ten years ago was not the original structuralist project of mapping out every possible configuration of story and discourse. Instead, feminist narratology took the form of "close reading." While classical structuralist narratology, in actual practice, contains brilliant passages of close textual analysis that illustrate its broader points (Gérard Genette or Gerald Prince can always be counted upon to tease as much meaning out of a phrase as the most subtle deconstructionist), it was never really about "close reading." Narratology claimed first to describe systems of literary meaning, and only secondarily—if at all—to interpret the meanings of individual literary texts. "What does it mean?" was never the motivating question for structuralist narratology; "*How* does it mean?" was the point of the original systems of narrative poetics. And the answer to that question was supposed to be deduced objectively.

Feminists interested in narrative theory invoked feminist epistemology to object that systems of meaning are never neutral, and that they bear the (gendered) marks of their originators. Hence, feminist narratologists never tried to replace the structuralists' systems with alternative systems of their own. Instead, feminist narratology focused on two kinds of projects that relied more on *both* close reading *and* historical context than structuralism ever did. These were (1) finding examples of narrative written by women that posed challenges to the categories of classical narratology, and referring to historical context to account for (the significance of) the gendered differences they observed; and (2) "reading in detail" as Naomi Schor so memorably called it, applying the analytic categories narratology made available to scrutinize texts very closely and arrive at gender-conscious interpretations of narratives. For feminist narratologists, "close reading" is still very much a "going concern" as we begin a new century.

Structuralist narratology is not so much a "going concern" in the beginning of the twenty-first century as it is a kind of intellectual backdrop, a set of terms and principles literary academics take more or less for granted in the pursuit of more overtly historical or "cultural" studies. Audiences at the Modern Language Association (MLA) no longer look puzzled if you talk about "diegesis" or an "extratextual" element: even a cultural studies crowd will recognize the terms. But cultural studies projects—because of their interdisciplinarity, because of the ambitious sweep of their theses, and because their authors are trained to eschew anything that smacks of a soulless, ahistorical "formalism"[24]—tend to avoid close reading. Just as I argued ten years ago that feminists needed to bring historical context into structuralist narratology, I argue today that we need to bring close reading—the skill narratologists, especially feminist ones, have always demonstrated almost in spite of themselves—into cultural studies.

By "close reading," I do not mean to invoke the old formalist method for conquering ambiguity and paradox to arrive at a unified meaning for a (great) text. Nor am I talking about the kind of thematic reading cultural studies scholars will occasionally do of a scene from a film or a TV show, generally to identify the ideological positions and contradictions being displayed. I am talking instead about a close analysis of form, a semiotics of *how* popular cultural texts convey meaning, rather than of what they mean to say. "Close reading" in its old-fashioned sense presents at least two obstacles for the scholar interested in popular culture: First, which text(s) should the scholar try to read closely, when every text of popular culture is by definition ephemeral? In doing a reading of, for instance, a scene from a soap opera, the critic cannot assume an audience's familiarity with that particular text, or even that the audience could retrieve the text if they wanted to check their own impressions against the reading. In this respect, close formal analysis of popular culture is necessarily different from the kind of work that feminist narratologists have so far done, in that we have generally assumed an audience that knows our texts, even when those texts are not, strictly speaking, canonical. The close readings in this book, for example, will not assume that my readers know all the details—or even the outlines—of the forty-plus-year-long narrative of *As the World Turns,* or that they have read the twenty volumes of Patrick O'Brian's Aubrey-Maturin novels or even the six volumes of Anthony Trollope's Palliser series. Nor will my close readings attempt anything like plot summary in the face of plots so utterly unwieldy as these. I analyze formal properties of plots without illustrating them at the level of detail that Genette, for instance, could achieve in his book-length study of *Remembrance of Things Past,* a work as canonical as it is voluminous. I try to strike a balance between what I believe my reader might want to know about the forms I am discussing and what I feel quite sure my reader does not want to know (if he or she did not know it already) about the specific details of popular cultural plots.

The question of canonicity raises the second difficulty for close readings of popular texts, one that Peter J. Rabinowitz, for one, has set forth very clearly.[25] As he has argued, "close reading" was invented as a means of evaluating and interpreting canonical texts, and it favors texts that are written according to its premises. A "closely read" popular text—one that operates conventionally, like a detective novel or television soap opera—can only end up looking bad. Based as it is on the canon, the method of course reinforces the canon. But as I have mentioned, the kind of feminist-narratological close reading I am advocating would not do close readings for the purpose of evaluating or even interpreting texts (as canonical close reading was supposed to do), but rather to describe their formal operations. As a feminist narratologist, I seek meaning not in the texts themselves, but in their interactions with and especially their actions upon audiences. As a general goal this is nothing new for cultural studies, but the attempt to base observations about audience on closely read segments of text is something cultural studies has not really ventured upon. I do close readings of individual installments of serial fiction and single scenes from episodes of a daytime soap opera, but not to find out what they mean. The meanings of the individual texts are secondary to the broader purpose of doing the close reading: uncovering the elements of form that signal the scene's participation in what I am arguing are gendered cultural processes.

Each of the chapters in this book identifies formal narrative techniques that elicit particular affective responses, charting the patterns of those techniques in a genre that carries strongly gendered connotations. In chapter 2, "The Cry: Effeminate Sentimentalism," I begin with a brief history and analysis of the genre of sentimental texts designed to inspire the "good cry," not the cathartic experience of tragedy, but the affirmative, triumphant, feminine "tears of joy." After citing some evidence of the prejudices operating in academia and in the mass media against effeminate crying over texts, I propose a narratology of the "good cry" that is neither tragic nor cathartic, uncovering the machinery by which texts work to make effeminate readers cry. This chapter and chapter 3 draw examples from among U.S. sentimental novels of the nineteenth and twentieth centuries, Hollywood films, and novels, television programs and commercials from the late 1980s, a period when U. S. popular culture seemed particularly focused on invoking the feminine "good cry."

Chapter 3, "The Cringe: Marriage Plots, Effeminacy, and Feminist Ambivalence" looks at the affective implications of novels and films structured by the marriage plot, considering them not so much in the light of sexual desire and consummation, but in terms of the many other (gendered) feelings associated with the middle-class conventions of courtship and marriage (for example, the anxiety associated with a pending change in one's social identity, or the anticipated thrill of acquiring new material possessions and changed economic status). I offer a brief recapitulation of the now-standard narrative theories of the marriage-plot formula, as well as an alternative analysis of the marriage plot as a technology not for enforcing heterosexuality, but rather for structuring effeminacy. Central to this chapter is an analysis of what it feels like to experience the marriage plot with a double consciousness directed simultaneously by feminism and effeminate feeling.

Chapter 4, "The Thrill and the Yawn: Antieffeminate Structures of Feeling in Serial Forms"—the only chapter of the book to address the structuring of antieffeminacy in popular culture—is the first of two chapters devoted to serials. I analyze serial novels by Anthony Trollope aimed at nineteenth-century mixed-gender audiences and Patrick O'Brian's Aubrey-Maturin series marketed to late-twentieth-century masculine readers, texts that are designed to capitalize on feelings of suspense and excitement while balancing readers' agitation against repetitions, redundancies, and formulaic plots. Making comparisons between the antieffeminate effects of serial fiction and of e-mail correspondence, this chapter offers a poetics of serial form as the basis for some speculations about the somatic effects of seriality on the initiated reader, and begins to sketch out a hypothesis of how serial adventure narratives structure emotional experience that is coded as not effeminate.

Chapter 5, "The Climax and the Undertow: Effeminate Intensities in Soap Opera," looks at the affective experience of long-term viewers of daytime television soap opera, a contemporary serial form that structures effeminate feelings to follow a wavelike pattern of feeling, endlessly reiterated until the series' demise. I trace the ambivalent relation of feminist television studies to soap opera, noting (and participating in) a recent change in the referent of "the viewers" from "them" to "I." Drawing on personal experience as well as on the reported reactions of participants in an AOL discussion group, I do an analysis of what it feels like to watch a continuing serial (*As the World Turns*, on the air since 1956) for as long as forty-three years. I track the "wave pattern" of emotional ebb and flow through a sequence of serialized episodes and through the responses of viewers in the on-line discussion group to demonstrate how soap opera performs as a technology of gender for effeminate viewers, males and females alike.

CHAPTER TWO

The Cry: Effeminate Sentimentalism

He longed to lay Amy's head down on his shoulder, and tell her to have a good cry.

—Louisa May Alcott, *Little Women* (1868–69)

Jo wanted to lay her head down on that motherly bosom, and cry her grief and anger all away; but tears were an unmanly weakness.

—*Little Women*

Gender Quiz: Guy or Gal? "I saw 'Little Women' and although I enjoyed it, I felt the movie would have been improved by an explosion or even a little irony."

—*Sylvia* comic strip (March 4, 1995)

A red-eyed Michael opened the door. . . . He led her into his bedroom and pointed to a chair. "Sit down and have a good cry. This woman is God's gift to romantics." He held up an album cover. . . . "Every faggot in town adores her."

—Armistead Maupin, *Tales of the City* (1978)

Like walking with a swing of the hips or talking with lots of hand gestures and fluid movements of the wrist, having a good cry signifies effeminacy. In British and U.S. mainstream culture of the nineteenth and twentieth centuries, weeping openly and emotionally—whether for grief, anger, frustration, sympathy, relief, joy, triumph, or gratitude—is an activity associated with girls and women, considered appropriate to their female frames and delicate feelings. Men cry, too, of course: if they are gay men, their tears are understood as part of the penchant they are supposed to share with feminine women for "making a spectacle" of their feelings;[1] if they are straight, they must be perceived as shedding "manly tears" or run the risk of compromising their reputations for masculine heterosexuality. To have a *good* cry, though, is to indulge in one of the perquisites of effeminacy, whether the person doing the crying is male or female.[2]

Not coincidentally—given the convergence of homophobia and misogyny in dominant culture even at the new century's beginning—having a good cry is also an embarrassing thing to do, especially when the weeping has been inspired not by a direct response to life experience, but by a narrative. The common names for genres that typically invoke crying carry connotations so negative as to require no comment: "tearjerkers," "sentimental drivel," "five-handkerchief movies," "women's weepies." Feminist film theory—with its psychoanalytically inspired tendency to read women's crying over films as a masochistic pleasure and films' manipulation of women's sentiments as a form of textual/sexual violence—has not done much to ameliorate the negative associations of crying over stories.[3] By contrast, gender-centered interpretation of nineteenth-century sentimental novels has recently taken some important steps toward the recuperation of readerly tears associated with grief, mourning, and loss.[4] But these studies overlook the positive grounds for crying that also inhabit sentimental texts. Tears of joy, of relief, and of triumph are as much a part of the effeminate audience's response to sentimentalism as are sympathetic tears of sadness—perhaps more. These tears represent a cry that is unequivocally "good," but that has received very little attention in studies of emotion.

Having a Good Cry

The paradox of the "good cry" has proven to be an embarrassment not just to literary and cultural critics, but also to social scientists developing the "mood management" model of audience response to popular texts. The idea of mood management is that audience members ought to be able to perpetuate a good mood, or get out of a bad one, by choosing entertainment that will cheer them up or calm them down. Reasoning from principles resembling those of the "rational choice" movement among economists, researchers such as Dolf Zillmann have grappled with the perversity of crying audiences' evident desire to cultivate negative feelings, without considering the differences the audience's gender identity might make in their assessment of what a "negative feeling" is supposed to be.[5] As Mary Beth Oliver has saliently pointed out, the mood management approach oversimplifies the dynamics of effeminate audiences' tears by taking it for granted that crying—every baby's response to hunger, loneliness, or fear, and many adults' expression of pain or grief—is always only a negative experience. Oliver summarizes the conclusions of the mood management approach, exaggerating only a little: "[Their] predictions paint a picture of tearjerkers that is clearly at odds with commonsense notions: Tearjerkers should be immensely unpopular, only tearjerkers that jerk no tears should be enjoyed, and only viewers who are emotionally insensitive or unfeeling should experience gratification in response to this type of entertainment" (318). The proponent of mood management might well ask: why would anyone choose to read a novel or see a film that might lead to crying?

To untangle the paradox, Oliver makes a useful distinction between "emotional reactions" and "feelings *about* emotional reactions," which she calls "metaemotions." Her detailed, quantitative study shows that feminine subjects report positive feelings about crying, finding pleasure and even satisfaction in the experience of textually induced tears. Taking a cue from Oliver and adding another dimension of analysis, we might think of the "good cry" in terms of metaemotion on both the personal and the cultural levels: Within the effeminate audience's response, there is the physical experience of the cry itself (the emotion or affect) as well as the meta-experience of that emotion (the crying subject's own attitude toward the activity of crying over books or movies); within the cultural context, there is also another level of metaemotion, the prevailing prejudice against such effeminate crying. Every crying subject's metaemotional experience of textual tears forms in response to the culture's metaemotion. As I move into a discussion of the cultural context of the "good cry" in contemporary U.S. culture, I am making a distinction that Oliver herself does not make, between "sad" or "tragic" narratives, on the one hand, and what I call "good-cry" texts on the other. I will argue that the "catharsis" model that has guided critical understanding of crying over tragedy does not hold for the tears induced by sentimentalism. As I see it, the culture's lingering embarrassment over having a good cry is grounded partly in a gynophobic and homophobic reaction to the effeminate connotations of textually induced crying; partly in modernism's philosophical and aesthetic recoil from the feminine associations of popular culture itself, and especially of sentimental popular culture; and partly in specifically modernist models of what crying does in and to the body of a reader.

When I speak of a prevailing prejudice against sentimentally induced tears, I am locating it in at least two centers of cultural power, the academy and the middlebrow mass media. The common prejudice against sentimentalism shared by these two entities complicates the pattern Andreas Huyssens (1986) locates in late-nineteenth-century America, "the notion that mass culture is somehow associated with woman while real, authentic culture remains the prerogative of men" (47). "Time and again," Huyssens reports, "documents from the late nineteenth century ascribe pejorative feminine characteristics to mass culture—and by mass culture here I mean serialized feuilleton novels, popular and family magazines, the stuff of lending libraries, fictional bestsellers and the like" (49). Huyssens traces the development of the modernist aesthetic as a gynophobic "reaction formation" against the feminine connotations of mass-cultural forms (53), and argues that the gendering of high and low culture persists throughout the modernist period, beginning a period of decline with postmodernism in the 1950s and 1960s. Interestingly, though, I find that in the later twentieth century, the mass media—by which I mean "popular and family magazines," syndicated newspapers, and other twentieth-century descendants of those very forms the late nineteenth-century culture denigrated as "feminine"—work hard to distance themselves from popular cultural forms that are specially marked as "feminine," such as sentimental novels and films or soap operas. Fans of these forms are perceived and portrayed as weak, excessive in their emotionality: in short, as effeminate. In this, the mass media work hand-in-hand with academic projects that habitually belittle effeminate pop-culture forms.

Indeed, the official pronouncements and unstated assumptions about sentimentality are surprisingly consistent from the mainstream media to the academy. Middlebrow magazines tell us, for instance, that when the audience of a high-art theatrical production weeps, the tears are the sign of a tragedy's power and validity: *Newsweek* says of Joseph Papp's production of *The Winter's Tale* that the actors "seem to be as overwhelmed as the audience, and tears are plentiful on-stage and off" (Jack Kroll 1989, 70). Had this remark been made about *Beaches* (1988), *The Color Purple* (1985), *Little Women* (1994), or *Stepmom* (1998), its implications would almost certainly have been negative. But *The Winter's Tale* isn't a sentimental Hollywood melodrama; it's Shakespeare. Therefore, "this frank, immediate emotional reality is one of the strengths" of the production, according to this arbiter of middle-class taste. If a popular text (especially a film) makes actors and audiences cry, by contrast, the press's typical reaction is to assign mechanistic, derogatory labels to it and to generalize about its "manipulative" characteristics.

As an example, consider an article for Gannett News Service by Julie Hinds called "Get Out Your Handkerchiefs" (the title alludes to the Bertrand Blier movie that parodies sentimental domestic dramas). Noting the surge in the 1980s of sentimental Hollywood films, Hinds quite unselfconsciously demonstrates every clichéd prejudice against the genre imaginable. All her quotations of authorities come from commentators who call such films tearjerkers and "weepers"; her own analysis refers to "getting all choked up" and "tugging . . . on . . . heartstrings." She explains that "women's weepies" have traditionally been "marketed at females, who received cathartic enjoyment out of watching someone else overcome tribulations." Never mind that the essentializing term *females* places her own resisting voice outside the realm of her sex. To provide closure for her article, she borrows a man's voice anyway, quoting a male critic who says of the sentimental effect: "That's really stupid. It doesn't ask the audience to do anything except get run over by a tractor." Hinds adds, "And bring a lot of Kleenex." Hinds's tone is light, her vocabulary slangy; her article is supposed to be amusing. But if the spectacle of the woman crying at *Terms of Endearment* (1983) or the 1980s remake of George Cukor's 1936 *Camille* (two of Hinds's examples) is funny, why shouldn't the audience at the Shakespeare play be open to similar ridicule?

Of course, feminist academics have been tackling the problem of the critical double standard now for over two decades. Within the academy, such critics have gone some distance since the 1980s toward "rehabilitating" sentimentality in certain contexts, particularly in nineteenth-century U.S. women's literature. Traces of the distaste for being made to cry still surface, however, in what even the most progressive critics say—or don't say—about sentimentality.

Beginning with the premise that a prejudice against sentimentality— and particularly against textually induced tears—pervades U.S. cultural criticism inside the academy as well as outside, I propose to locate the roots of that prejudice in a powerful but seldom-challenged model of the relationships among emotions, the body, and texts. Certainly, the dismissal of sentimentalism, not to mention the mode's perverse habit of persisting in U.S. culture despite that dismissal, can be traced to many influences having to do with the intertwining histories of gender, class, and aesthetics. One of those influences, I will argue, is a persisting idea of the body as a repository of "real" emotions, a reservoir of passions that high art (such as classical or Shakespearean tragedy) can legitimately tap into and that sentimental novels or films can divert for exploitative or commercial purposes, thus rendering the resulting affect somehow less "authentic."

Among the implications of this "reservoir" model of the body and its relation to texts is the idea that the experience of elite audiences (like the crowd at the Papp production) is more genuine, more "frank [and] immediate" than the emotional experience of the popular audience having tears wrung out of its eyes by such "exploitative tearjerker[s]" (as one review has it) as *Stella,* the remake starring Bette Midler of King Vidor's *Stella Dallas* (1937) (Fine 1990, A5) or other classic "weepies" like *Terms of Endearment* or *Dark Victory* (1939). I believe that this differentiation between the physical experiences of elite audiences and popular ones is a distinction based on gender, born of a collective cultural recoil from effeminacy. Academia's theoretically sanctioned response and reaction to sentimentality is, after all, constructed: it arises not from some "natural" aversion to certain intrinsically objectionable textual strategies, but from a historically specific prejudice against sentimentalism per se. As I have suggested in the previous chapter, this prejudice has its roots in modernism's assumptions about what the "nature" of the body, and its relations to emotions, is supposed to be.

Sentimentalism and Sexism

As anyone can see from the account in my Preface of my experience of being made to cry by the sentimental devices underpinning the virulently antisentimental *Wag the Dog,* I am no more immune to the prejudice against crying over texts than I am to the power of texts to make me cry. For unambivalently enthusiastic reactions to "having a good cry," I must turn to evidence provided by other scholars' research, such as Oliver's study (1993) of the metaexperience of crying among feminine audiences, or Helen Taylor's survey (1989) of admirers of *Gone With the Wind,* or Barbara Sicherman's analysis (1989) of the reading habits of a Victorian American family. Despite the ambivalence of my own experience of the "good cry," I resemble the subjects of those research projects in that the relative familiarity or newness of a text seems to have no bearing on my response if the text happens to be one of those that "get to me." Like the women Taylor interviewed, whose copies of their favorite novel are "now well thumbed [and] tearstained" (35) and who gather ritually to cry together over repeated video viewings of the film, I can expect to be made to cry, quite consistently, by certain texts. Some passages of *Uncle Tom's Cabin* and of *Little Women* invariably bring tears to my eyes, although I have quoted, commented upon, and taught them dozens of times—as do some scenes near the end of *King Lear.* I am embarrassed, though—humiliated even—to admit (in a context as formal as an academic publication) that texts so different in reputation have so similar an effect on me.

And am I not typical, at least among contemporary feminist academics? I pride myself on my analytical toughness, my ability to take apart any text and propose explanations for how and to what ends it was put together. Yet I am perfectly capable of sitting before a screen—watching perhaps *Terms of Endearment* (which I loathe), perhaps *It's a Wonderful Life* (one of my favorites), or even watching a Disney movie (I cried while watching Disney's 1999 *Tarzan* in the theater with my little boy; the crying started sooner and lasted longer during the second of our three theatrical view-ings of the film, triggered by Phil Collins's by-then familiar theme song for the film, "Two Worlds, One Family") or a television commercial (espe-cially that infamous AT&T ad from the late 1980s, immortalized by the tag line, "He just called to say, 'I love you, Mom'"; or the blissed-out slow-motion images of families getting dressed in "cotton, the fabric of our lives"; or the euphoric assertion from GE that "We bring good things to life")—and experiencing a physical response identical to what I feel every time I reach the end of Shakespeare's great tragedy, when Lear and Cordelia are reconciled. Even the most crassly sentimental text can make me cry. And I have resented it—as I suppose you do, too—if you are will-ing to acknowledge similar susceptibilities. Tragedy is one thing, but for readers who have been trained under the modernist aesthetic of defamil-iarization and alienation effects, there is something objectionable about obviously commercial texts that so readily and mechanically arouse emo-tion: it's too easy; it must not be "authentic." But the insights made pos-sible by postmodernism, which allow for skepticism about traditional criticism's assumptions that some feelings are "genuine" or authentic and others are not, put us in the position of being able to ask: Is not all inte-rior experience to some degree socially or culturally constructed? Why, then, should we perpetuate this modern distinction between tragedy and sentimentality, this prejudice against sentimental effects in art?

For some critics, as for the Gannett movie reviewer, the prejudice is a nat-ural one. You can pick up any nonfeminist reference work on nineteenth-century American fiction almost at random to find evidence of this. Witness Herbert F. Smith's *The Popular American Novel: 1865–1920* (1980), which, for example, only briefly mentions that famous inspirer of feminine tears, *Little Women* (1868), to acknowledge the popular success of this novel "and the various sequels it spawned." Notice how the repellent metaphor removes the agency behind the novel's reproduction from the woman writer, attributing it to the text itself, which is supposed to have dropped its sequels into the world by some biological process, as a fish drops eggs. Louisa May Alcott does get grudging credit from Smith for "having dealt with middle-class life," but that gets canceled out by Smith's next (and final) pro-nouncement on the sentimental domestic novelist: "her use of realism to increase sentimentality was too perverse to be favored by any but children and gushing girls" (47). The formulation is odd, since realism in other lit-erary contexts is a value for Smith. But he explains early in his book that sentimentality is a "disease," and that the "discriminating critic" must act as a "pathologist" to trace its symptoms and—presumably—to cure it (19), even where it coexists with realism.

The dismissive sexism of Smith's position on nineteenth-century women writers and their readers is so blatant as to be, in itself, uninteresting. His remarks are useful here, though, in at least three ways. First, his metaphor of infection transmutes the text into a body, which has the effect of deflecting attention from the literal body of the person (the woman, he assumes) who holds the book and reads. Second, this thinking about texts in terms of bodies is, as I will explain below, a negative variation on nineteenth-century American critics' ideas about the way texts and sentiments operate. And third, Smith's negative assumptions— perhaps predictable in their context—also operate more subtly and more surprisingly in works of criticism analyzing sentimental texts in less openly prescriptive terms.

According to Nina Baym's (1984) comprehensive analysis of nineteenth-century critics' criteria for judging fiction, "all good novels were expected to contain pathos," a term "used by reviewers to denote an emotional response . . . characterize by pity, sadness, or sorrow—'to dissolve the heart in tears'" (*Novels, Readers, and Reviewers,* 140). Baym emphasizes that the reviewers she studies took an "affective" approach to the novel (149), and that their attention was focused not on a work's thematic content or specific techniques, but rather on its emotional impact upon individual readers (142). In their view, the best novels elicited laughter and tears. Baym locates a pattern of medicinal metaphors among individual reviews, and attributes them to "a conception of the novel as a substance taken into the body, there to work an effect beyond the reader's control" (58). For the nineteenth-century reviewer, then, sentimental passages in a text were part of the text's machinery for "working an effect" in a reader's body, and if that effect were one of "pathos," the result would be to the benefit of the reader. Consider the contrast with Smith's staunchly modern metaphor, which overlooks the reader's body (literally present though it is in any act of reading) and transforms the text into a metaphorical body in its place. In Smith's model, sentimentality is the disease infecting the body of the text, whereas in the nineteenth-century model, textual pathos was the medicine for the body of the reader. For Smith, the heroic medical efforts of the critic/pathologist who expunges the disease take center stage; the crying body of the girl reading Alcott gets erased, with a sneer, from the picture.

Certainly Baym is very careful to acknowledge the historical contingencies at work in the evaluation of fiction, and though she wryly declines to "spend much time on the issue of how it might be that people enjoyed being made to feel bad" (141), she scrupulously resists the kind of dismissal of nineteenth-century values that Smith practices. In an earlier book (1978) she cautions against using sentimental as "a term of judgment rather than of description," because such judgments, usually negative, "are culture-bound": the critic of a later time who uses the term disparagingly is refusing "to assent to the work's conventions" (*Women's Fiction,* 24). But even Baym is not immune from her era's negative assumptions: why does she see her subjects as enjoying "being made to feel bad"? No excerpt that she cites from her nineteenth-century reviewers indicates that her subjects found anything "bad" in the feelings they are writing about. In other words, to avoid culture-bound dismissal of the popular nineteenth-century novel, we need to assent to the conventions of the reading process, as well as of characterization, story, or style.

Far less willing than Baym to accept the conventions of her subject matter is Janet Todd, who has chronicled the philosophic and aesthetic history of British sentimentalism in *Sensibility: An Introduction* (1986). Todd's attention to the productions of the cult of sensibility yields a thorough and helpful survey of that eighteenth-century mode of writing. But she takes it for granted that twentieth-century readers and viewers, with their "taste . . . for the ironic and self-reflexive in literature" must necessarily find the mode "repellent" (142). She means, of course, *elite* twentieth-century readers and viewers. Skipping ahead to Victorian America, she concludes her book with the famous passage from *Uncle Tom's Cabin* where Eva dies what Todd chooses to call a "public and redemptive but politically impotent" death (149). As I will argue more fully below, seeing Eva's death as "politically impotent" requires limiting one's view to what happens inside the fiction, rather than attending to the fiction's impact upon actual readers and their potential involvement in political change. But for now, let us focus on Todd's negative attitude toward the sentimental response per se.

Todd concludes her book with what appears to be a set of alternatives for how readers might respond to sentimentality. Close analysis suggests, however, that Todd's alternatives boil down to something like this: "You can hate sentimentality, or you can hate it." Labeling the style of Eva's deathbed scene "overcharged," Todd remarks: "Depending on period and personality, readers of such prose can join Godwin and Coleridge in lamenting the prestige of feeling in culture, or they can with Doris Lessing's character in *The Sentimental Agents of the Volyen Empire* (1983) see such flamboyant sensibility as a destabilizing addiction and a glamorous corruption; they can turn away in embarrassment or they can choke and cry" (149). The parallel structure of this sentence makes for an elegant and resonant ending to Todd's book, but its logic is not clear. "Readers . . . can . . . (1) lament . . . or . . . (2) see . . . addiction and . . .

corruption; they can (1) turn away . . . or . . . (2) choke and cry." The syntax suggests that sentimentality can (1) embarrass us, as it did the male Romantics, or it can (2) appear to us in the light of addiction and corruption, as it does in Lessing's antisentimental novel. Hanging on at the end of the sentence is the second above, which does not parallel the first and has no place in the sentence's logic: "they can choke and cry." Is that what readers do, who see sentimentality as addiction and corruption? Is there no alternative for the *other* reader who finds something positive, or possibly even empowering, in the sentimental response? Significantly, Todd draws upon the same set of disease metaphors that Smith uses to talk about textual sentimentality, though this time it's the reader's body that is subject to addiction and corruption. Though Todd acknowledges response must depend "on period and personality," she nevertheless leaves no room in her period for the effeminate personality who might like sentimentality.

Todd's aversion aligns her with commentators who see sentimentality as politically impotent, a position she attributes in particular to Mary Wollstonecraft (132). The idea that someone who cries over representations of injustice, poverty, and pain will be necessarily helpless to do anything about their "real-world" referents is pervasive in modern criticism, as we have seen in the case of the movie reviewer who asserts the sentimental text "doesn't ask the audience to do anything." But the idea is peculiarly unsuited to the experience of nineteenth-century middle-class Americans, especially women. Alice Hamilton (1943), whose family's reading is the subject of Barbara Sicherman's research, reports that her father considered her Victorian American mother to be subject to "sentimentality" which "he hated"; her mother's favorite literature contained decidedly "pathetic" material (including such canonically respectable texts as Gray's *Elegy* and George Eliot's *The Mill on the Floss,* a novel whose final pages I have never been able to reread without crying). But if Mrs. Hamilton could cry over a book, she could also take responsibility for action. The daughter repeats the mother's motto in the face of social injustice: "There are two kinds of people, the ones who say 'somebody ought to do something about it, but why should it be I?' and those who say 'somebody ought to do something about it, then why not I?'" (32); Hamilton places her mother in the second camp. For a woman holding such attitudes, the emotional affect aroused by a book was its means of making its subject matter personal to her: the sentimental response was a sign that the fictionally represented experience was registering in her body. Evidently the act of crying was not, for her, a vent for passions that might more productively have been spent elsewhere; instead, it fanned the flame of what her daughter admiringly calls her "enthusiasms" and "indig-nations." Mrs. Hamilton's behavior, then, contradicts the assumption Todd shares with the movie reviewer, who, as we have seen, claims females "received cathartic enjoyment out of watching someone else over-come tribulations."

Feminist literary and cultural criticism has gone a long way, in the past two decades, toward acknowledging that sentimentality had political and cultural work to do in nineteenth-century America. Granting the warrant to such projects, Jane Tompkins (1985) argued eloquently in the 1980s about *Uncle Tom's Cabin,* among other sentimental novels, that it "repre-sents a monumental effort to reorganize culture from a woman's point of view" (124), and that while it obviously never fully achieved that goal, it did have an enormous cultural and political impact on its large, enthusi-astically responsive Northern audience. Tompkins attends primarily, though, to the text's representations of weeping—and to the assumptions about religious "truths" its audience presumably held—without really talking about the audience's own propensity for crying. Certainly, one can more readily come up with data for a study of how crying is depicted in texts than for an inquiry into how crying gets inspired by them. Despite the ontological difficulties presented by the question, however, I will show, in the third section of this chapter, that representations of weeping are not necessarily the only, or the most potentially effective, means that sentimental texts use to inspire readers' tears. I contend, too, that to focus on representations of weeping in the text, rather than acknowledging the crying reader in one's analysis, is to evade the referent of our culture's dis-comfort with this phenomenon: the flesh-and-blood body of the crying woman (or "gushing girl") who reads. Tompkins is responsible for dis-seminating the idea that modern criticism categorically dismisses texts that "do something" to readers. But even the unembarrassable Tompkins (it took a lot of intestinal fortitude to write "Me and My Shadow," which exposes the critic's own emotional experience of academic life in an unprecedentedly physical way) turns aside from the spectacle of crying readers.[6]

A project following close on the heels of *Sensational Designs* in its efforts to see popular nineteenth-century novels in a rehabilitative light, Philip Fisher's *Hard Facts* (1987) looks more deliberately than Tompkins's book at the physical, emotional effects sentimental texts can have on their willing readers. For Fisher, the act of crying is part of the reader's partici-pation in the novels' project of "familiarizing" historically marginal and oppressed groups, such as slaves, children, or the insane. Following a model proposed by Jean-Jacques Rousseau, Fisher reduces several of the tear-inspiring scenes in *Uncle Tom's Cabin* to a basic paradigm: an immobilized witness watches a monster violently separate a victim from the victim's loved one; unable to intervene, the witness has no recourse but to weep in dismay and frustration. *Uncle Tom* is full of reiterations of this pattern, different from Rousseau's model only in that the characters' tears well up during narrations of the sad events as well as during their direct enactment. (I am thinking, for instance, of the scene where Senator Bird's whole household weeps while Eliza tells them her story, or the scene where young George Shelby is overcome with tears when he tries to write to his mother about Tom's death.) Fisher suggests that the reader of these scenes is in a position analogous to Rousseau's witness: unable to intervene in the oppression, to bridge the gap between text and world, a reader who weeps is, according to Fisher, venting helpless frustration.

Taking sentimentalism on its own terms, Fisher's theory positions itself as a defense of the mode within its historical and cultural context. As he puts it, "by limiting the goal of art to the revision of images (or oppressed persons or groups) rather than to the incitement to action, sentimentality assumes a healthy and modest account of the limited and interior consequences of art" (122). Embedded in this conclusion, however, are at least two strong signs of the prejudice against sentimentalism that is so much more clearly in evidence in other critics' work. First, Fisher's model may account for the "tears of defeat" associated with sentimentality, but it does not address the "tears of triumph" (James Smith 1973, 15, 56), the "good cry" that dominated sentimental reading experiences later in the nineteenth century, that persist in the Hollywood tradition of the "weepy" film, and that contribute, for that matter, a large part of the emotional impact of *Uncle Tom* itself. Second, Fisher's theory supports the idea that crying over fiction equals political impotence. His argument forces him to relegate to a footnote the truism that *Uncle Tom's Cabin*, in his words, "is perhaps the single most effective political work of art in the history of literature"; his note can only shrug this off as a "paradox" (182). In other words, Fisher's model works beautifully in theory, but faced with the historical fact that crying readers did take action after having read the novel, the theory falters. I suggest the problem is the critic's reluctance to look too directly at the moving, acting bodies of the crying audience, as well as his model's reliance on the notion that textually induced tears are always cathartic. As I have suggested in my Introduction, the theory of catharsis, influential as it has been in criticism since Aristotle's formulation of the idea, is not always the most appropriate working model for explaining the experiences of nineteenth-century readers.

A Narratology of Good-Cry Techniques

The "good cry," then, is not like "cathartic weeping": it does not purge or drain an effeminate body's feelings; rather, it rehearses and reinforces them. It is not inspired by original artistic genius or aesthetic merit; instead, it can arise in response to a set of familiar and highly formulaic narrative practices.

In place of the perhaps expected catalogue of scenes where characters are depicted as weeping, or even of interpretations of individual texts in the "good-cry" tradition, what follows is a narratology of the techniques commonly employed in sentimental narratives to evoke readerly tears. In identifying these technologies of affect, I am not referring to presumed authorial intention or to narratorial assertion, but rather to the physical impact these techniques can have on susceptible readers who are familiar with the genre of "good-cry" narrative through exposure to nineteenth-century sentimentalism or to its descendants, the Hollywood "chick flick" and the U.S. daytime soap opera. As I compile this list of techniques, I consult my own habitual reaction to each of them, and I rely on the consensus of those students, friends, and colleagues who say they recognize the "good-cry" experience I am pointing to. While the list mainly limits its illustrations to examples from such recognized classics of American sentimentalism as *Charlotte Temple, Uncle Tom's Cabin,* and *Little Women* and such notorious "tearjerkers" as *It's a Wonderful Life, An Affair to Remember, Terms of Endearment,* and *Sleepless in Seattle,* each technique has its analogs in such late-twentieth-century "good cry" novels directed to effeminate audiences as Alice Walker's *The Color Purple* or Amy Tan's *The Joy Luck Club,* as well as in other films that make audiences cry, from *Stella Dallas,* to Douglas Sirk's *Imitation of Life* (1959), to *Stepmom.* In describing seven patterns I discern in the narrative discourse of sentimental novels, then, I orient each toward its customary effect upon the susceptible and cooperative reader. Those seven patterns follow:

1. Such novels as *Charlotte Temple, Uncle Tom,* and *Little Women* employ narrative voices that draw upon the connotative power of poetic devices to heighten the emotional impact of the prose. This is what undergraduates like to call "flowery writing." To be sure, there is nothing intrinsically emotional about poetic language. But these devices would have been familiar to the nineteenth-century woman through the lyrics of hymns, the poems in keepsake books and literary collections, and the commemorative poetry family members wrote to console one another for bereavements. In each of these cases, poetic language would carry heavily emotional connotations through its association with spirituality,

friendships, family relationships, and the loss of loved ones to death or emigration.[7]

The most common poetic devices in sentimental novels are the most purely mechanical. They include, for instance, alliteration: "A sudden sickness seized her; she grew cold and giddy, and putting it into her husband's hand, she cried . . ." (*Charlotte Temple*, 90); "But a bird sang blithely on a budding bough, close by, the snowdrops blossomed freshly at the window, and the spring sunshine streamed in like a benediction over the placid face upon the pillow—a face so full of painless peace that those who loved it best smiled through their tears. . ." (*Little Women*, 392). Equally mechanical is the reliance upon punctuation that emphasizes emotional affect in the narrator's utterances (including exclamation points, dashes, and italics occurring outside the passages of dialogue).

Less obviously, sentimental prose plays with poetic tropes of presence and absence to subvert the logical relations between the imagined world of the diegesis and the physical world inhabited by the reader, blurring the lines between them for emotional effect. For instance, sentimental narration can use apostrophes to bring the characters into the same plane of reality as that inhabited by the readers, whom the narrator also frequently addresses: "Even so, beloved Eva! Fair star of thy dwelling! Thou are [*sic*] passing away. . ." (*Uncle Tom's Cabin*, 383). This self-consciously poetic style is, of course, what Todd means when she calls the language of Eva's deathbed scene in *Uncle Tom* "overcharged."

The Hollywood equivalent of "flowery writing" includes melodramatic acting styles inherited from silent film, repetitions of musical themes familiar to the intended audience, and use of specifically sentimental instrumentation and voicing in the soundtrack's musical arrangements. For all its *mise en scène*'s emphasis on realist detail in the creation of the world of Bedford Falls—for all the fussily recreated interiors of homes and offices, all the pointed ordinariness of the costumes and props—Frank Capra's *It's a Wonderful Life* (1946) exemplifies a style of classic melodramatic acting recognizable from films made decades earlier and from the stage plays they emulated. When George Bailey (James Stewart) encounters the nightmare version of his hometown's alternate reality, his increasing horror is photographed in the starkest black-and-white contrast, and his facial and physical expressions are extremely distorted, melodramatically grotesque; when he sobs out a prayer on the snow-covered bridge, discovers "Zuzu's petals" in his pocket, and then runs home joyously to his wife and children, his incarnation of despair and relief is exaggerated to the extreme. If "good-cry" moments in later films are less obviously melodramatic in their style, they build on melodrama's tradition of rendering emotion as something overtly visible. A memorable example is the deathbed scene of Emma (Debra Winger) in James L. Brooks's film of the Larry McMurtry novel, *Terms of Endearment* (1983). The scene is dominated by an excruciating close-up of Emma's youngest son, crying at her bedside—it is repeatedly and mercilessly intercut with the continuous take of the parting dialogue between Emma and her two boys, in which their facial expressions are much less vivid than in the close-up. For me, it is impossible to look at the anguish on that little actor's crying face without tearing up. The point of the scene—like that of the last scenes in Capra's movie—is the agonizingly beautiful trope of familial love, figured in a plot climax where the prospect of extreme loss comes together with intense gratitude for present emotional ties. The cry this spectacle evokes may not "feel good," but that does not make it any the less a "good cry."

Not just the visible, but also the audible effects of a film can place it in the good-cry genre. Music is perhaps Hollywood's most obvious equivalent to such poetic effects as alliteration and apostrophe. Quotations of musical motifs—familiar to the audience either from earlier moments in the film or from the culture surrounding the production and reception of the text—can carry similar emotional connotations to those borne by poetic devices borrowed from sentimental verse or from hymnody. *It's a Wonderful Life* uses a Christmas carol, "Hark the Herald Angels Sing" along with the song associated with mainstream U.S. holiday gatherings of friends and family, "Auld Lange Syne," to heighten the sentiment of the happy climax in the Baileys' home by tying it to nostalgic wishes or memories the audience is assumed to hold dear. Even when a soundtrack's themes are original, good-cry movie music favors arrangements that emphasize sentimental aural cues like high-pitched strings and children's singing voices. *An Affair to Remember,* directed in 1957 by Leo McCarey, even includes soft-focus footage of a children's choir performing under the heroine's direction. The sequence is seemingly endless, and embarrassing for more reasons than one (for instance, the tragically crippled heroine must direct the group from a seated position; her enforced sedentariness is awkwardly relieved when the only two black children in the group jump down from the risers to perform a tap-dancing break), but—like the violin strains that swoosh throughout that film and all the Hollywood romances it resembles—these high-pitched sounds carry connotations of the cry. It is not a coincidence that people sometimes pantomime a violin performance when they want to make fun of friends who are narrating their own present woes.

2. The embellished style runs parallel to a theme common in sentimental novels (and their close relative, Gothic novels) suggesting representation, in the form of mere language, is inadequate to convey the depths of emo-

tion the characters and narrator are presented as feeling. This theme is transmitted in the narrative discourse, both through scenes of characters' being
pushed beyond speech by their feelings, and through narrators' remarks to
the authorial audience. In *Charlotte Temple,* for instance, the characters are
frequently too overwhelmed by emotion to be able to utter words: "his
heart was too full to permit him to speak" (24); even more often, their bodies are overpowered by their emotions, and they "fall prostrate [or senseless]
on the floor" (16, 48, 85, 109). The sentimental narrator reinforces this
theme by frequently claiming that the emotions she must report cannot be
rendered in language, but must be "unnarrated," as Gerald Prince (1982)
calls the technique of naming that which cannot be told in a story: "[she]
gave vent to an agony of grief which it is impossible to describe" (*Charlotte
Temple,* 86); "I don't think I have any words in which to tell the meeting of
the mother and daughters; such hours are beautiful to live, but very hard to
describe, so I will leave it to the imagination of my readers" (*Little Women,*
187). Such unnarrated passages are a signal to the reader to fill in the blank
with the emotions for which the narrator cannot find words. The cooperative reader must follow the cues and take an active part in co-creating the
scene's affective power.

   Although unnarration is less common in Hollywood film than in sentimental fiction, *An Affair to Remember* provides a lovely example of how
a good-cry movie can heighten the emotional impact of a fictional
moment by placing an action outside the frame. Just before their first kiss,
Nicky (Cary Grant) and Terry (Deborah Kerr) have been discussing
tears—he remarks that she has been weeping while she looks at the view
from the ocean liner's deck (though the camera reveals no sign of tears on
her face) and she says, "That's what beauty does to me." When Nicky
moves to kiss Terry, she backs away and proposes that they walk; together they descend a staircase, holding hands. The camera shows them from
below as they walk downstairs: their feet, legs, clasped hands, and torsos
come into view. Then, just as his head moves into the frame, she pauses,
her head still out of sight, and she pulls him back up the stairs so that the
top edge of the image cuts off both their upper bodies at the waist and his
hands are no longer visible. Sufficient time elapses for a long kiss, as her
hand grasps the railing, rises to touch him, and then comes back down
into the frame. Finally, the two descend the staircase and go on playing
the scene. I would call this kiss "unnarrated," and would point to it as evidence that good-cry texts achieve heightened emotional effects as much
by refusing to represent moments of intense feeling as by attempting
directly to represent them.

   3. Sentimental narrative discourse requires a particular handling of

"internal focalization," Genette's (1979) term for the technique of limiting narrative perspective to a single character's consciousness, despite the
fact that the character does not speak the narration. Scenes in sentimental novels and films tend to be focalized either through victims (such as
the many slaves separated from their families in *Uncle Tom,* the over-
worked and underappreciated George Bailey in *It's a Wonderful Life,* and
the long-suffering Emma in *Terms*) or triumphant figures who have for-
merly been represented as oppressed (such as each of the March daughters in her little moment of glory, as when Meg receives praise from her
husband, Jo gets a piece of writing accepted for publication, Beth receives
the gift of a piano, and Amy accepts Laurie's marriage proposal). This
focalization invites the reader to participate emotionally from the subject-
position of the oppressed, in the diegetic good times and the bad.
Sentimental novels can use embedded first-person narratives to achieve
this effect, as when Cassie narrates to Uncle Tom the miserable story of
her life as a "quadroon" slave sexually abused by her "master" (*Uncle Tom's
Cabin,* 514–22). More often, the "omniscient" narrative focus simply
shifts to the perspective of the sufferer, rendering the scene as he or she
sees it, for instance, in the chapter of *Little Women* called "Amy's Valley of
Humiliation," in which the youngest of the heroines is physically pun-
ished at school. As Fisher has pointed out, the focalization in sentimental
narrative sometimes comes through sympathetic intermediary figures who
are not, themselves, directly oppressed—such as Eva in *Uncle Tom*—but
it is seldom if ever granted to those who oppress the protagonists in the
fictional world. This careful limiting of the narrative point of view to
those who suffer and triumph after tribulation can effect a powerful pull
on the sensations of a susceptible reader. In sentimental novels, moreover,
the "good cry" is much more often evoked by scenes of triumph than by
scenes of sadness: it is not Eva's death that inspires the cry, but her conviction that she is going to a "better place"; Beth March's death scene is
notorious for making readers cry, but so is the earlier scene in which Beth
does not die while her mother is out of town, but survives for a mother-
daughter reunion.

  Attention to the role narrative focalization plays in the affective dynam-
ic of reading fiction and film is important, as it presents a challenge to the
idea that readers sympathize with suffering characters when they can
"identify" with them.[8] As a concept within psychoanalytic interpretation
of texts, identification puts the crying reader in a position of enjoying
pleasures that are specifically masochistic. If we think about the reader's
tears as, in part, a consequence of the text's technical arrangement of
perspective, rather than as a reflection of the reader's consciously or sub-

consciously feeling that the miserable or triumphant sufferer is "just like me," however, audiences' participation in sentimentalism becomes more positively performative, less revealing of some presumed hidden truth about the readers' "real feelings."

4. The narrators of sentimental novels frequently use earnest, direct address to a narratee, calling upon him or her to recognize parallels between lived experience and the situations represented in the fiction. This, of course, is the notorious "preachy" tendency of sentimental novels that so many twentieth-century readers could not abide. Direct address to the reader is, however, central to the sentimental novelists' project, in that it does *not* rely on the actual audience's "identification" with characters to be the grounds for readers' taking the fiction seriously. The sentimental narrator (usually an example of what I have called elsewhere the feminine "engaging narrator") enforces comparisons between a flesh-and-blood reader's experience and characters' experiences which readers might not "naturally" have made on their own.

Rowson does it often: "My dear young readers, I would have you read this scene with attention, and reflect that you may yourselves one day be mothers. . . . Then once more read over the sorrows of poor Mrs. Temple, and remember, the mother whom you so dearly love and venerate will feel the same" (*Charlotte Temple*, 54). Stowe does it even more often: "In such a case, you write to your wife, and send messages to your children; but Tom could not write" (*Uncle Tom's Cabin*, 228); "And if you should ever be under the necessity, sir, of selecting out of two hundred men, one who was to become your absolute owner and disposer, you would, perhaps, realize, just as Tom did, how few there were that you would feel at all comfortable in being made over to" (476). Any given reader's ability to answer such an appeal would depend on that reader's willingness to step into the role constructed by the narrator's utterance (does Rowson's reader have to be female, to feel the agony of a mother's potential loss? Does Stowe's have to be male, to answer to the threat of freedom curtailed?). But those readers who could respond, whether on a literal or an imaginative level, might be effectively invited to participate in the represented emotions.

Earnest direct address to the audience is one good-cry technique that does not seem to have carried over from the sentimental novelistic tradition into Hollywood film. The cinematic diegesis appears to be at the same time so overwhelming and so fragile as not to admit the kind of affective interruption sentimental novelists use to such powerful effect. Direct address to the audience in conventional Hollywood film is more often employed as a comic or ironic device akin to the antifeminine storytelling mode I have called in *Gendered Interventions* (1989) "distancing narration." While the effect is broadly comic in films like Mel Brooks's *Blazing Saddles* (1974) and John Hughes's *Ferris Bueller's Day Off* (1986), I admit to being as much moved as amused by Woody Allen's use of the device in *Annie Hall* (1977). Allen as Alvie Singer repeatedly turns to address the camera, in order to draw the viewer's attention to a question of interpretation, or to appeal to the audience's knowledge that other characters have acted and spoken as Alvie thinks they have, in spite of their denials of what we, like Alvie, have seen and heard for ourselves. No one would call *Annie Hall* a "good-cry movie," and I doubt it makes anyone's list of classic chick flicks. Still, it is my favorite Woody Allen movie because of the way it blends its metafictional self-consciousness with sentimental techniques, particularly the nostalgic repetition of musical motifs (Diane Keaton's and the soundtrack's renditions of "Seems Like Old Times," for example, or the unusual screen appearance of Paul Simon during the same era that "Still Crazy After All These Years," another version of a story like Annie and Alvie's, was a hit), as well as the direct appeal to the audience to participate in the film's narration.

     5. The sentimental plot emphasizes close calls and last-minute reversals, either for better or for worse. Charlotte Temple drops dead only moments after her father finally finds her; young George Shelby arrives just too late to save Tom; Eliza escapes over the frozen Ohio River with no time to spare; the March girls' father gets home from the Civil War on Christmas Day. The actual reader who allows him- or herself to become absorbed in the fictional world can experience emotional jolts when expectations are either dashed or suddenly fulfilled, and those jolts can bring on tears— especially when the unexpected outcome brings a sense of "what a relief!" In filmic plots this technique is as common as it is in novels; film editing, too, can enhance or even enforce the effect. When Steven Spielberg uses the camera trick described in my preface, to assure the audience of *Saving Private Ryan* (1998) that its hero will not be killed, then kills him off in the penultimate scene, his technique is amplifying the effectiveness of dashed expectations in making the audience cry; when the wife of Matt Damon's character reassures him that his own life has compensated for the hero's sacrifice, the sense of relief amplifies the cry. In this example, the "better" of the good cries would be the final one, the cry of relief and triumph.

     While good-cry films will rely on temporarily dashed expectations to inspire an audience's tears, they almost always end "happily," steeped in that sense of triumphant relief. Nora Ephron's *Sleepless in Seattle* (1993)— the good-cry film that does more than any other to thematize the good

cry itself—makes broad use of last-minute reversals and improbable coin-
cidences in its plot, as the hero and heroine played by Tom Hanks and
Meg Ryan repeatedly almost meet, but always just keep missing each
other. The film also refers overtly and repeatedly to *An Affair to
Remember,* quoted in *Sleepless* three times as a movie that makes female
viewers cry. Women and girls cry while they watch it and even when they
talk about it; men and boys are puzzled or bored by it, and make fun of
the effeminate response by pretending to cry at the end of their favorite
hard-boiled war movie *The Dirty Dozen* (1967). Directly borrowing from
the climax of *Affair,* Meg Ryan's Annie asks her future love to meet her at
the top of the Empire State Building; the audience who knows the
McCarey film will expect the meeting to fail, as it does for Nicky and
Terry, and will not be surprised as Meg Ryan and Tom Hanks miss each
other's elevators by seconds. Still, the last-minute close calls build to the
good-cry relief effect of the conclusion, when Annie returns to the observation deck. None of it is plausible; none of it is surprising; none of it is
original—indeed, the effectiveness of the moment depends on its intertextual resonance, not just with the movie it quotes, but with the whole
good-cry plot-reversal tradition it emulates.

6. Contrary to received wisdom, sentimental texts do not present two-
dimensionally "stereotyped" characters, but rather rely on characterization
that mixes traits to work against the types that have been established in
the text (or in the culture). This strategy works together with the unexpected reversals of the plots to produce readerly tears. An example of such
an exploded character type would be the respectable, emotionally
repressed, publicly powerful middle-class patriarch—such as Senator Bird
in *Uncle Tom's Cabin* or Mr. Laurence in *Little Women*—who turns out,
against his type, to be capable of forming an emotional bond with a slave
or a child.

Consider, for example, the scene in which Beth astonishes her family
by overcoming her shyness (up to this point, her dominant trait) and vis-
its Mr. Laurence to thank him for the piano he has sent her:

> If you will believe me, she went and knocked at the study door before she
> gave herself time to think, and when a gruff voice called out, "Come in!"
> she did go in right up to Mr. Laurence, who looked quite taken aback, and
> held out her hand, saying, with only a small quaver in her voice, "I came to
> thank you, sir, for—" But she didn't finish for he looked so friendly that she
> forgot her speech and, only remembering that he had lost the little girl he
> loved, she put both arms round his neck and kissed him.
>
> If the roof of the old house had suddenly flown off, the old gentleman

wouldn't have been more astonished; but he liked it—oh, dear, yes, he liked it amazingly!—and was so touched and pleased by that confiding little kiss that all his crustiness vanished; and he just set her on his knee, and laid his wrinkled cheek against her rosy one, feeling as if he had got his own little granddaughter back again. (60)

Here, both Beth and her benefactor behave against type, as do all the protagonists in *Little Women* and in *Uncle Tom* in their moments of triumph. Examples of other "good-cry" techniques I have cited (for instance, the direct address, "If you will believe me"; the alliteration, "lost the little girl he loved," and ejaculation, "he liked it amazingly!"; the focalization through two characters who have up to this point been represented as emotionally repressed or suppressed; the sudden reversal coming through Beth's unexpected kiss) add the stylistic prompts for the readerly tears.

Good-cry movies with romance plots employ the device of characters acting against their established type, as do domestic good-cry dramas. As Nicky the cynical rake in *An Affair to Remember,* Cary Grant is called upon to contradict his established type by visiting a saintly, ancient grandmother and by joining the pious Terry as she kneels to pray inside the tiny chapel in the "perfect world" of his grandmother's garden. His decision in the tearful denouement to stay with the crippled heroine further confirms his character's capacity to act against type. In a less romantic, more domestic example, Shirley Maclaine's Aurora in *Terms of Endearment* has, throughout the film, treated her daughter Emma with nothing but prickly criticism and disapproval. When she sits, grief-stricken, at Emma's deathbed, and even more when she fiercely defends her late daughter against her resentful grandson's imprecations, Aurora's uncharacteristic behavior carries much of the good-cry impact of the film's conclusion. Indeed, characters in good-cry films behave against type with a regularity so predictable as to disprove the assumption that the emotional effect of these character reversals has anything to do with surprise. In good-cry narratives, a type evidently implies the coexistence in the same character of its own antitype; the playing out of complications that result from this formula contributes to the good-cry effect.

7. Though they always depict scenes of grief and suffering, sentimental novels counterbalance them with scenes of joy and triumph, albeit bittersweet. Although I have chosen the scene of Beth's kissing Mr. Laurence almost randomly from among dozens of "good-cry" scenes in these novels that would equally well illustrate the principle, it turns out to be a paradigmatic example of why the "good cry" over a "weepy" text like *Little Women* is more triumphant than it is tragic or despairing. To be sure, the reference to the lost granddaughter is sad (as is the repeat-reader's knowl-

edge that Beth, too, will die before the novel's end), but if the mode of the passage is not comic, it could almost be described as antitragic: the rebirth and recuperation of the patriarch's tender feelings, the happiness and emotional generosity of the living little girl, the unexpected blessing of their coming together over his gruffly offered gift are the incidents that dominate the scene's emotional tone, leaving little room for pity and far less for anything like terror. The susceptible reader who cries at this scene—or indeed, at the scene of Beth's demise or of Eva's death and presumed ascent into heaven—is not purging negative emotion in a cathartic process, but rehearsing and reinforcing affirmations of joy.

The plots of sentimental novels rely upon repeated moments, like this scene between Beth and Mr. Laurence, which serve to "mythologize" the fictional experience in that they draw upon effeminate culture's store of cherished beliefs and—contrary to the perhaps painful evidence of readers' own lived experience—make those beliefs seem to come true. In cases where the subject matter is as politically charged as it is in *Uncle Tom's Cabin,* this can mean reducing situations of extreme moral and logistical complexity, if only momentarily, to epiphanies of pure simplicity. This last and most powerful of the techniques of sentimental narrative discourse can account—as Fisher's model cannot—for the "tears of triumph" that dominate *Uncle Tom's Cabin* and *Little Women,* as well as the "tears of defeat" that appear to have prevailed in an earlier era among the readers of *Charlotte Temple.*[9] When—in *Little Women*—Mr. Laurence's dead granddaughter seems to have returned to him in the form of Beth, when Meg and Jo are reconciled after a long period of bickering, when their father returns from the war just in time for Christmas; or—in *Uncle Tom's Cabin*—when Eliza and George are reunited at the Quaker settlement on their journey to Canada, when the bigoted Vermonter Ophelia realizes she loves the slave Topsy, when Eva or Uncle Tom dies with the most confident expectation of going to heaven, does it make any sense to imagine the weeping reader as experiencing frustration? This reader is "having a good cry," an affirmation of the mythology being represented in the text: family affection *does* transcend death; sisters *are* friends forever; true love *will* prevail; courage *will* be rewarded; affectionate domestic relationships *will* put an end to racist oppression—oh, it *is* a wonderful life!

Crying Over *The Color Purple*

With this lapse into sarcasm (for which I apologize: earnest as I tend to be, I find it nearly impossible to discuss the good cry without rhetorically rolling my eyes, those same eyes that sentimental narratives can cause to fill with tears), I mean to invoke that most notorious of all cry-inducing scenes in a classic Hollywood movie, the moment near the end of *It's a Wonderful Life* when the depressed and frustrated George Bailey suddenly realizes how much better the world has been for his existence in it, and how beautifully the circumstances of his life actually fit his hopes and ideals. Who can resist the lump in the throat that comes with watching Jimmy Stewart push through the jovial crowd of affectionate neighbors, greet his delighted wife, and run ecstatically up the stairs of his home, joyously crying out "Kids!" as he embraces the family his nightmare has taught him to appreciate anew? Like the gang at the bar in *Cheers,* in the episode where they all make fun of the idea of crying over *It's a Wonderful Life,* then find themselves moments later with their heads tilted up toward the bar's TV monitors and their faces streaming with tears, I find it difficult to invoke that movie's message—or indeed any of the affirmed myths of sentimentalism—without being sarcastic; the legacy of modernist (not to mention postmodern) irony makes that impossible. The association of exalted, ecstatic, or optimistic feelings with the darker undersides of bourgeois mythologies (with racism, classism, homophobia, and nationalism especially) makes them suspect, false, "sentimental" in the most pejorative sense of the word.

The 1980s—the same decade that made crying over *It's a Wonderful Life* a byword for sentimental response, the decade when *Cheers* defined "must-see TV" on Thursday nights—also produced and received the twentieth-century text I see as one of the strongest challenges to prevailing prejudices against "having a good cry": Alice Walker's *The Color Purple* (1982). Walker's novel is unabashedly sentimental: it makes readers cry. As a result, its political and social efficacy has come into question. If the novel makes readers cry, can it do positive, antiracist, antihomophobic, feminist cultural work? I argue that it can, and that an appreciation of the good-cry tradition can illuminate how that is possible.

For me and for many of my students and fellow readers over the past fifteen years, the last letter in Walker's epistolary novel functions to invoke a good cry reminiscent of the climactic moments of *Little Women* and *Uncle Tom's Cabin,* as well as the end of *It's a Wonderful Life.* Looking specifically at the technologies of affect I identify in the narratology of sentimentalism I have proposed above, I would attribute the final scene's affective impact to the ways it uses focalization (point 5, above) to underscore the novel's affirmation of effeminate mythologies (point 7). The novel's epistolary form both complicates and clarifies my model of good-cry techniques.

Epistolary fiction (the form of *The Color Purple*), with its shifts in narrative voice and in temporal perspective, brings the affective mechanics of focalization into especially vivid relief. As the letter writer relates each segment of the story, she has access only to her own consciousness (like any conventionally realist first-person narrator, she cannot read other characters' minds, but can only report their actions and expressions, both verbal and physical). Her perspective is even more strictly limited, however, than that of the homodiegetic narrators of novels that are not epistolary, in that she only knows as much about the story as she *can* know at the time of composing the letter: she has not yet "lived" beyond the moment at which she is writing, and hence cannot foreshadow, in her narration, what is to happen after that moment.[10]

Since Samuel Richardson's *Pamela,* epistolary novelists have made the most of this technique's ability to build suspense and to heighten the affective impact of fictional narratives. Like Pamela, Celie does not know, in moments when she is writing in fear and anger, that her tribulations will end happily; unlike Jane Eyre, for example, she does not tell her story with the double consciousness (and the inevitably ironic distance between the "I" who speaks and the "I" who experiences) that comes from lifelong retrospection.[11] Of course, epistolary narratives are usually written retrospectively, but the retrospection is in pieces, arranged serially as it were, rather than spanning the length of the diegetic time represented within the narrative. Hence, the telos in epistolary fiction is distinct from that of nonepistolary narrative, in that the epistolary narrator can reflect no sense of his or her final outcome in the narration, even if the author has used other means to establish foreshadows. The effect, for the willing or cooperative reader of the sentimental epistolary novel, is a heightened physical experience of reading that can be readily enlisted in the service of the good cry. The actual reader is "in the moment" with the epistolary narrator; the potential for detachment that is available to the authorial audience of retrospective or otherwise distanced narration is not available in epistolary form.

Critics commenting on *The Color Purple* take it for granted that this novel inspires readerly tears with moments of intensely rendered grief (as when the adolescent Celie mourns the two babies that were born to her and then brutally taken away; or when she is separated from Nettie, seemingly forever; or when she encounters the beautifully Amazonian Sophia, physically and emotionally diminished by her time in jail). But for me, the biggest cry comes at the novel's end, with a burst of joy peculiarly foregrounded by the focalizing effect of the epistolary form. The first fifty letters in the novel are addressed by Celie to "Dear God." Up to that point, the narrative form more closely resembles a diary than an epistolary fiction; the letters to God are a chronicle of Celie's isolation, inspired by her supposed father's injunction against her reporting his repeated, incestuous rapes: "You better not never tell nobody but God" (11). At the novel's formal turning point, the diary form gets interrupted by eight of the letters Nettie has written to Celie from Africa, hidden until this point by Celie's abusive husband, Albert. Celie's rage against Albert and against that rapist who, she learns from Nettie's letters, was *not* in fact her own father, leads her to conclude that God "must be [a]sleep" (163). At this point, with a third of the novel still to go, Celie changes her address from "Dear God" to "Dear Nettie," and though Nettie's subsequent letters are not answers to the letters Celie addresses to her, the remainder of the text takes the form of a correspondence (although it is undelivered and undeliverable) between the two sisters.

As commentators have observed, Nettie's letters serve the thematic purpose of broadening *The Color Purple*'s geographical and political horizons to include Africa and to connect that continent to Celie's little corner of the U.S. South. The interpolation of Nettie's letters also serves a narrative function, though, as the letters provide Celie with an embodied narratee. Nettie's existence as narratee becomes the textual sign of Celie's relief from isolation, her coming into community as she comes out into her lesbian sexuality with Shug. When Celie grumbles to Shug about her religious disillusionment, Shug offers Celie an alternative view of God: "I believe God is everything, say Shug. Everything that is or ever was or ever will be. And when you can feel that, and be happy to feel that, you've found It. . . . She say, My first step from the old white man [image of God] was trees. Then air. Then birds. Then other people" (178).

As Celie renders it in a letter to Nettie, this scene's initial significance is in its romantic dimension, since it brings Celie closer to Shug. The Celie who relates this conversation cannot know how its vocabulary will return in the novel's last letter, or how the words' significance will shift, and so she cannot foreshadow its significance. The susceptible reader will be taken unawares, in the novel's final pages, by the scene's reprise.

Because the epistolary form focalizes the narrative through Celie's present state of feeling in each of her letters, the sudden happy ending does indeed carry heavy affective clout. But what makes me cry in Celie's last letter is not really the "happy-ending" events. It is not the unexpected return of Nettie, whose narrative trajectory has flouted verisimilitude by reuniting her in Africa with Celie's two lost children and bringing them back, with their adoptive father (Nettie's own new husband), to live with Celie again. It is not the mother-and-child reunion that accompanies the sister's return. Nor is it Celie's own newfound good fortune in having a place to welcome them to, having inherited the home her birth-father has left to her, thus solidifying the financial independence she has begun to establish with her pants-making business. For me, it is not the situation that inspires the good cry—really, the situation is almost laughable in its literal implausibility. The scene's emotional effect is brought about through the confluence of the narrative discourse with the novel's passionate endorsement of mythologies central to femininity (mythologies about sisters, mothers, children, and financial self-sufficiency, for instance), in the address of Celie's last letter. After having addressed fourteen consecutive letters to "Dear Nettie," Celie starts her last letter with a completely new beginning: "Dear God. Dear stars, dear trees, dear sky, dear peoples. Dear Everything. Dear God. Thank you for bringing my sister Nettie and our children home" (249). That passage gets me every time. The way Celie's voice crosses the diegetic boundary, to include me in her address ("dear peoples. Dear Everything") and, in so doing, to assert my inclusion in Celie's newly minted concept of God; the way her address brings into being a moment of pure community embracing not just Nettie, as the previous letters had done, but all the characters and even me; the unmixed joy and triumph of the moment of ecstatic enunciation always make me cry.

Walker's novel is not a "high-culture" text; if it has made its way into the Women's Studies university canon, it was a best-seller first. Jane Shattuc (1994) is notable among the feminist commentators who have speculated about the racially inflected politics of middle-class women readers' crying over Walker's novel. But the reputation of *The Color Purple* as a good-cry text got complicated in fascinating ways when Steven Spielberg made a Hollywood film out of it in 1985. Reviews of the film blasted it for sentimentalism (*Newsweek* complained that "sometimes the sentimentality quotient is allowed to reach dangerously toxic levels" [December 30, 1985]) and for antimale prejudice, conflating Spielberg's text with Walker's original in their dismissal of its antiracist and prowomanist themes. Reviewers in politically progressive journals, especially, focused on the film's jubilantly happy ending as its most objectionable feature. The *Christian Century* brings to mind James Baldwin's classic objection to the emotionalism of *Uncle Tom's Cabin,* putting it bluntly: "Spielberg is wealthy today because he gives us what we want. Never one to miss a potential market, he knows that we would rather feel than think. Pull out all the stops, batter our brains out with a little violence, a little sex, a little revenge, a little religion, and we will leave the movie thinking that we have been part of something significant. Unfortunately, the problems between men and women, blacks and whites, the powerful and the

powerless cannot be cured by a good cry" (vol. 103, April 2, 1986). Of
course not. But what the reviewer misses is that the good cry at the end
of Spielberg's movie draws on a misreading of the resolutions of the conflicts of racism and sexism invoked by Walker's novel. In this misreading,
the *Christian Century* is not alone; the *Progressive* similarly elides the different technologies of sentiment operating in Spielberg's version and in
Walker's: "The melodramatic happy ending of *The Color Purple*, in which
an unlikely concatenation of circumstances makes it possible for all its
previously separated characters to be joyously reunited, stretches the
credulity of the most confirmed optimists. Yet here it is that Spielberg
faithfully renders the book. In an act of sheer perversity, he omits or adul-
terates so much of what is most expressive and original in the novel and
then realizes its weakest part with great fidelity" (vol. 50, February 1986).
As any undergraduate who has recently read the novel and then watched
the film can tell you, Spielberg's adaptation actually makes a significant
revision in the resolution of Walker's plot: in the last scene of the novel,
Albert (the "Mr. ————" who had oppressed Celie in her role as his
reluctant wife) is sitting companionably on the porch with Celie and their
mutual love, Shug, sewing shirts and making conversation, taking his
place in the utopian community created in the end by the return of Celie's
blood relatives. At the end of Spielberg's film, Albert stands aloof in a
field, glowering from a distance at the joyful reunion. If the film suggests
that "the problems between men and women" can be "cured by a good
cry," the novel insists that only a profound subversion of gendered and
sexual norms can bring about anything like a cure for those problems. In
Walker's version, Albert has to learn to sew, to accept his former wife's lesbian relationship with his former lover, to laugh with them over sexual
difference (by carving a frog as a gift for Celie, who has remarked to him
that all men, with their pants off, look like frogs to her); similarly, Celie
has to overcome her stereotypically effeminate penchants for dependency,
abjection, and sexual competition with other women. Like the president's
handlers in *Wag the Dog*, Spielberg knows all about the technologies of
feeling that bring on the good cry. What his *Color Purple* doesn't compre-
hend, though, is what *Wag the Dog* communicates in spite of itself: the
positive values of effeminate culture (and I don't mean dependency, abjection, or any of the more painful elements of what Helena Michie
has called sororophobia) can bypass the cynicism of sentimentalism-for-
profit; the cry of the "gushing girl" can be a good one.

   To those who ask, "What's 'good' about 'the good cry'?" I respond (without sarcasm, now) that the ideals of sentimental culture—the affirmation
of community, the persistence of hopefulness and of willingness, the belief

that everyone matters, the sense that life has a purpose that can be traced to the links of affection between and among persons—are good ideals. If manipulators of public sentiment do what the fictional president's handlers do in *Wag the Dog*, and deploy the narrative techniques of the sentimental tradition in the service of nationalism, capitalism, and commercialism, that does not drain the techniques themselves (or their potential affective impact upon actual audiences) of value. As I have mentioned, becoming more conscious of how those techniques achieve their effects does not render readers immune to them, but it can offer us the opportunity to affirm "feelings" that constitute what is worth preserving from cultures of effeminacy.

For Stowe and for Alcott, establishing and reinforcing the patterns that continue to underpin effeminate culture today in the United States, to make a reader cry would be to make something real happen. And that something continues to happen to susceptible readers, whether they are encountering *Little Women* or this century's versions of those narrated domestic mythologies, most often taking the form of melodramatic films or television programs. In the twentieth century, crying—under any but the most extreme circumstances of personal triumph or defeat—was coded as weak, childish, something for gushing girls to do. I think a twenty-first-century perspective can allow us to see that it was not a coincidence this association developed during a period when those texts which formally induce crying were being systematically devalued by critics in the academy and in the popular press. If we could put aside the prejudice against "having a good cry" over a book or a film, we would be in a position to envision a truly inclusive cultural poetics, where the evaluative standards of past eras might no longer have the power to exclude difference and diversity in descriptions of texts, or of the audiences who receive them. To resist thinking of catharsis as an essential or natural explanation for the relation between the body and the text would be a positive step in that direction.

And what about the sentimental audiences of the present century, those persons (male or female) who, perhaps partly unwillingly, can still "choke and cry" the effeminate tears evoked by these technologies of affect? I have sketched the beginnings of a list of mechanisms U.S. texts use to make audiences cry, but I do not offer this list to actual audiences as a prophylactic against the sentimental effect. Creatures of culture that we are, we may not be in the position to change the patterns of affect resulting from our participation in that culture: witness my reaction to the technologies of affect in *Wag the Dog*. Emotion is there, in the body, structured—perhaps—by the kinds of cultural forms I am describing, but impervious to rational control or intervention. Emotion we cannot choose to change, but we can make choices about metaemotion, or what we think about how we feel. If we are devotees of the good cry, we don't have to be embarrassed when our tears remind us that we are living in bodies, and that we are repeating the experience of generations of gushing girls before us. If the container/catharsis model has indeed led to a view of crying audiences as alienated, isolated, and disempowered, I suggest we take a cue from the Delsartean model, which saw emotion as corporeally, publicly, even communally produced. As for the effeminate readers who love "having a good cry," I envision a community empowered by a relationship to sentimental texts that is both visceral and self-aware, fully conscious of how strategies "get to us," and free to enjoy the physical act of crying. If we can dispel that sense of embarrassment and isolation associated with textually induced tears, our potential for participating in the transformation of culture and society will be that much more powerful.

CHAPTER THREE

The Cringe: Marriage Plots, Effeminacy, and Feminist Ambivalence

I was once sitting unsuspecting in my office when a student burst in, her face flooded with tears. This was normally a very cheerful person, a funny, bawdy, ex-hippie ex-nurse-midwife who'd come back to school to study English and write. I thought that something awful had happened, one of her kids killed? Wrong. She was crying because she'd just finished reading *Jane Eyre* for my class and was "so *happy* for Jane and Rochester!"

—Naomi Jacobs

When *thirtysomething* premiered on ABC in the fall of 1987, Jane Shattuc and I were both thirty-two years old. Junior faculty members at the University of Vermont, we did not know each other well, but the same demographics that marked us as the new nighttime serial's ideal target audience—white, middle-class, upwardly mobile, (over)educated, politically progressive, East Coast–based, Midwest-born, professional women—almost overdetermined our friendship. That we would begin to talk was inevitable, particularly in a small New England college town where the addition of "feminist" to our other identity markers placed us, at that time, in a tiny minority within our community. *Thirtysomething* was to become one of the instruments by which we came to measure our sameness and our differences, as women and as feminists.

We came together over an episode in that first season: Hope (the series's married, childbearing, part-time professional heroine) endures a visit from her mother, a houseguest returning briefly to Philadelphia from her retirement home in Phoenix. Vaguely, we remember the issues the episode raised: Hope resists her mother's attempts—through criticizing Hope's behavior, through offering to buy Hope a dress—to continue shaping her daughter's adult identity; Hope gets angry, treats her mother rudely, repents, and apologizes. Alone in our single-women's apartments, Jane and I watched this episode; independently, we had very similar responses. Both of us cried, hard and aloud, during the reconciliation in the last five minutes of the show; both of us, immediately after it ended, called our mothers (Jane's in Indiana, mine in California); and both of us, despite having been moved, felt embarrassed and annoyed by the fact that this commercially produced text had succeeded in manipulating us into taking the advice of those AT&T commercials (also capable of making us cry) to "reach out and touch someone," or to spend money on a long-distance call.

At work the next day we talked about this and were struck with the resemblance in our responses. In subsequent weeks, we would watch new episodes alone, and call each other at eleven on Tuesday nights, as often as not still in tears, asking, "Did you feel that one? Did it get you?" Still irritated, but fascinated by the appeal this crying experience held for both of us, we tried to understand the source of the feelings. Jane attributed her own crying during that first episode to frustration over the all-too-familiar scenes of mother-daughter conflict, but she concurred with my observation that the tears flowed most freely from elation over the resolution, the closure, the confirmation of the belief our culture (ironically enough, in both its traditional and its feminist manifestations) had engrained in us that differences between generations of women *can* be elided, and that the blissful mother-child unity psychoanalysis tells us existed before the mirror stage *can* be glimpsed again in moments of emotional epiphany. For me, the tears signify the relief that comes with the resolution of a powerful narrative line, moving from possession, to loss, to restitution. Call it "boy meets girl / boy loses girl / boy gets girl," or call it "daughter loves mother / daughter fights with mother / daughter reconciles with mother," that narrative line is the same. And its resolution brings about irresistible feelings which I would attribute to our accumulated cultural and individual experience of countless stories following that same line: fairy tales, television dramas, romance novels, "realistic" novels, gossip, films. Particularly when it centers on a heterosexual pairing, that pattern has come to be known as "the marriage plot."

As we developed and cotaught a course at UVM called "Having a Good Cry," Jane and I found our canonical example of the good cry to be the convention of crying at weddings, a tradition observed, often unwillingly, by countless American women despite our individual opinions about the actual desirability of the bourgeois expectations that wedding vows represent. We watch the couple take their vows, we know that for this moment—if for this moment only—they genuinely mean it when they say "I do": the speech act of taking the vow makes it so. And yet we know, from experience and observation, that the perfect embodiment of the ideals represented in wedding vows must inevitably begin to crumble, even as the couple turns to walk back down the aisle. "It's so beautiful," the crying spectator often says at weddings: "it," at the moment the couple speaks that vow, is the myth of American marriage taking momentary concrete form. But at that same moment, the spectator who is crying holds an awareness that this ideal is indeed a myth, and that once the couple is outside the safe space of ritual, the ideal will not exist in this almost tangible, crystallized way again. There is a sense of cringing, then, that accompanies the good cry we experience at weddings, a tincture of pain that accounts for its being a cry, not a giggle or a belly laugh. The cringe is associated with the inevitably provisional closure every wedding represents: at the end of the marriage plot, "boy gets girl," and the story is over, but for flesh-and-blood brides and grooms the moment must pass.

I see the marriage-plot pattern—and its associated emotional impact—as culturally instilled, not naturally present, and yet I believe it does function as a deep structure, not only in the narratives we are continually processing (in novels, on television, in movies), but also in the psychoanalytic account of basic human desire. For me, the "elation" part of the good cry comes with that familiar feeling of closure this narrative pattern habitually gives us; the "frustration" part comes with the gap between the gratification fictional closure brings and the uneasiness I feel at the infinite open-endedness of personal experience. But for me, neither the elation nor the frustration is experienced as specifically sexual, despite the erotic connotations of the vocabulary I am using here ("gratification," "elation," "frustration") and despite this narrative pattern's association with stories of a man and a woman "ending up together." Everyone knows the marriage plot is structured by sex, and is, at some level, experienced as an emotional analogy to sex. But like the "good cry" that so often accompanies narrative resolution, the marriage plot is gendered, too, in ways that do not necessarily connote or invoke sexuality. Performing a very close reading of the Julia Roberts film, *Pretty Woman*—too close for comfort, close enough, even, for discomfort—can untangle some of the intertwined threads of gender and sexuality in the effeminate response to marriage plots.

Reading Too Closely for Comfort

"Consider more closely," Silvan Tomkins suggests, "the tumescent male with an erection.

> He is sexually excited, we say. He is indeed excited, but no one has ever observed an excited penis. It is a man who is excited and who breathes hard, not in the penis, but in the chest, the face, and the nose and nostrils. But

such excitement is in no way peculiarly sexual. The same excitement can be experienced, without the benefit of an erection, to mathematics—beauty bare—to poetry, and to a rise in the stock market. Instead of these representing sublimations of sexuality, it is rather that sexuality, in order to become possible, must borrow its potency from the affect of excitement. The drive must be assisted by affect as an *amplifier* if it is to work at all. ("Affect as Amplification," 146)

Already we are close enough for discomfort: a look this close at the excited body in the context of academic reading makes me—for one—uncomfortable, as I immediately assume that no matter what Tomkins claims he is talking about, the gist of the passage must be primarily sexual. I don't even need to invoke "Freudian symbols" to be directed by the language of "the tumescent male," "erection," and "penis" to move from the literal level of the picture Tomkins evokes to a psychoanalytic reading of the language that follows. Who could resist assigning sexual connotations to the unaccountable eruption linking mathematics and poetry—"beauty bare"—and to the stock market's "rise"? Who could avoid arguing that even (or especially) when Tomkins disavows a necessary identity between excitement and sexual arousal, his writing almost parodically exhibits the very sublimation of sexuality he seeks to refute? When you note that Tomkins returned to these images in other writings using almost the same language (at a symposium twelve years earlier, Tomkins said, "No one has ever observed an excited penis. It is a man who is excited and who breathes hard, not in the penis, but in the chest, the esophagus, the face, and the nose and nostrils" ["Affect as the Primary Motivational System," 103]), who could resist concluding that this is a classic case of the return of the repressed?

Consider more closely, though, what Tomkins is saying—I mean, what he believes himself to be saying. What if he is right? What if "excitement is in no way peculiarly sexual"? What are the implications for a literary criticism whose close-reading practice has for decades been suffused with the conflation of readers' arousal and sexuality, usually expressed in terms of "desire"? Narrative theory, in particular, continually reverts to the trope of "desire" in discussing the emotional relation of readers to texts. As Peter Brooks (1985) so influentially put it, "Desire as narrative thematic, desire as narrative motor, and desire as the very intention of narrative language and the act of telling all seem to stand in close interrelation" (54); certainly they have come to stand in interrelation so close as uncomfortably to crowd out any competing notion of the feelings evoked by reading. Brooks was right, I think, to locate the warrant for his model in the literary texts it describes, for instance the European nineteenth-century novel, whose "ambitious heroes . . . may regularly be conceived as 'desiring machines' whose presence in the text creates and sustains narrative movement through the forward march of desire" (39). Never mind, for now, what Susan Winnett (1990) taught us to think about the phallocentrism of the way Brooks formulates that "forward march," nor what Judith Roof (1996) points out about its inexorably heterocentric trajectory. What happens to our close-reading practice if we step even further away from Brooks than Winnett and Roof, move down the road Tomkins points out, and detach the affective experiences of reading from the sexually defined notion of desire?

Consider more closely, now, the reader's body. I can speak with authority (albeit discomfort) only about my own, and I am necessarily blind to the unconscious operations of the drives that motivate its actions: I only know, as we say, what I feel. One thing I do know is that I have never experienced an orgasm while reading. This is not to say that in the course of reading I never found myself in a state that led me to take other actions to reach that conclusion, but coming is not—for me—a physical effect of reading. Therefore, I understand all the literary-critical language of desire and climax as metaphorical. The building excitement of a sustained narrative line is like sexual arousal, but it is not sexual arousal; gratification at the climax of an intensely experienced narrative is like an orgasm, but it is not an orgasm. My project is to enlist Tomkins's approach as an analogue to a literary criticism that would look more closely at what the body is doing while the reader reads, rather than always automatically making the metaphorical move into the language and analysis of sexual desire.

Consider more closely, then, some manifestations of the body's affective experience in Tomkins's own text that are not, specifically, sexual. Tomkins differentiates himself from a psychological tradition he traces from Plato to Freud, by making a distinction between "primary drives" and "primary affects." For Tomkins, a psychology based on "drives" is too limited and limiting of what he thinks of as "freedom of will"; his alternative to what he sees as Freudian determinism is a model of emotions understood in terms of their physical manifestations ("affects"), rather than their unconscious motivations ("drives"). To identify affects, Tomkins does close readings not of the subject's dreams or discourse, but of the face. As Sedgwick and Frank explain, "More than the place where affects are *expressed,* Tomkins shows the face to be the main place in the body—though by no means the only one—where affect *happens*" (30). By the end of his career, Tomkins had "distinguished nine innate affects," each of them associated with a particular facial expression:

The positive affects are as follows: first, *interest* or *excitement*, with eyebrows down and stare fixed or tracking an object; second, *enjoyment* or *joy*, the smiling response; third, *surprise*, or *startle*, with eyebrows raised and eyes blinking. The negative affects are the following: first, *distress* or *anguish*, the crying response; second, *fear* or *terror*, with eyes frozen open in fixed stare or moving away from the dreaded object to the side, with skin pale, cold, sweating, and trembling, and with hair erect; third, *shame* or *humiliation*, with eyes and head lowered; fourth, *contempt*, with the upper lip raised in a sneer; fifth, *disgust*, with the the lower lip lowered and protruded; sixth, *anger* or *rage*, with a frown, clenched jaw, and red face. ("Affect as Amplification," 142–43)

Collaborators and competitors of Tomkins have disputed the exact number of affects (some claim there are eleven; Tomkins himself began with a list of only eight), but—from a literary-critical point of view—it does not seem important to know whether this list is accurate or complete. As I have argued in my Introduction, what does seem important to me is the idea that emotion need not be understood as an interior essence expressed through the face, but that it could be seen as performative. If smiling, crying, trembling, and sneering are not windows on an interior state of feeling, but are themselves the constitutive performance of feeling, then we could make some drastic alterations in our understanding of the relation between reading and feeling. What if reading narratives is not motivated by a "drive" or "desire"; what if it does not reflect a more or less veiled or indirect acting out of an interior emotional state; what if the smiles, tears, tremors, and sneers evoked by narratives are themselves what make up the emotional component of the reading experience?

For feminist criticism, thinking about the reader's affective relation to narrative texts in terms of desire has been particularly compelling with reference to the marriage plot. To reach closure, the feminocentric marriage plot has to move from the action of "girl meets boy, girl loses boy" to the conclusion of "girl marries boy," or at least "girl elicits gesture from hitherto reluctant boy suggesting that he will, in the future toward which the diegesis gestures, offer to marry her." Following the metaphoric reasoning of desire-centered narrative theory, feminist critics have typically read the telos of marriage as the telos of heterosexual climax: if the heroine and hero get married, they will have sex; the readers' desire to see the marriage come about is understood as the readers' desire to see the protagonists come together sexually which—for the reader—will be, metaphorically speaking, to come. Readers who are addicted to marriage-plot narratives (whatever form those narratives may take: Harlequin romances, *People* magazine bios, mainstream Hollywood films, classic Victorian novels, Shakespearean comedies) follow a more or less predictable affective trajectory as they consume each new iteration of that plot: if the affect is understood as (sexual) desire, the trajectory follows that familiar parabola of mounting arousal gratified in the end by the climax of closure.

Short of "immasculating" themselves to identify with this stereotypically masculinist model of desire, however, what are effeminate readers getting out of their readings of the marriage plot? Feminist criticism has taken important steps over the past two decades in the direction of finding alternative story lines, resistances to closure, new endings, and new teleologies that would be more compatible with models of female sexuality (whatever that might be), but these alternatives do not account for the persistent popularity of marriage-plot narratives among effeminate readers; if desire is really the motor driving narrative, the marriage plot always ends up enforcing effeminate readers' complicity in their own sexual and cultural subjugation. Under this rubric, the marriage plot can only ever be oppressive or banal; to be sure, antiheterocentric reading strategies have recently produced some pretty compelling accounts of the marriage plot as inevitably just boring. Abject, melancholic, masochistic—these are the inexorable emotional end points of a desire-based model for effeminate reading of the marriage plot.

For me, though, the marriage plot elicits mixed feelings—and if boredom is not usually one of them, I don't think desire is, either. If I observe what the marriage plot does to my body—the physical signs of feeling it typically evokes—and look to Tomkins's list of nine basic affects for names to attach to those feelings—a list that excludes desire—I find excitement, enjoyment, shame, and sometimes (though not usually) surprise. Taking a cue from Tomkins's assertion that excitement need not necessarily denote sexual arousal, I am interested in looking at the patterns of affect underpinning marriage plots that may diverge from, or even entirely undermine, that old clichéd parabola of phallocentric heterosexual desire.

Discomforts of Reading *Pretty Woman*

To illustrate the idea I will take a close look at that worst of bad object choices for feminist critics, *Pretty Woman* (1990). If, as a feminist reader, I feel shame in getting excited about marriage plots, *Pretty Woman* brings me to the point of humiliation. No text makes more vivid for me the double experience of negative feminist political critique and positive physical readerly affect that always accompanies my reading experience as a lover of the marriage plot; at the same time, *Pretty Woman* provides the clearest example I can find of why the marriage plot is not necessarily a story about heterosexual consummation. The pattern of affect the marriage plot sets up—the alternation of excitement and shame—is, I would argue, partly constitutive of effeminate emotional experience in mainstream U.S. culture; it may indeed mirror or stand metaphorically for sexuality, but it does something more—and, I am arguing—something different from that: it puts the effeminate reader's body through a pattern of affective paces that add up, over a lifetime of reading, to the experience of gender itself.

Let me begin, just to get it over with, on the source of my shame at enjoying this movie, the negative feminist critique of *Pretty Woman*. Ideologically, the film's gender politics are as backward as they can be, remarkably consistent with the nineteenth-century American cult of domesticity. *Pretty Woman* divides the world into the masculine sphere of commerce and politics (Richard Gere's character, Edward, is the million-aire corporate buyout jock, with the financial power to acquire and dis-mantle companies, the political clout to tell Senate committees what to do, and the means to employ and outfit a courtesan to be at his "beck and call" for a week) and the traditionally feminine sphere of emotion, domes-ticity, consumption, and pleasure. The protagonist, Julia Roberts's Vivian, and her colleague, Kit, are the women who have crossed that divide between the public and private spheres in the only way the film can imag-ine women as commercial beings: they are prostitutes. But Vivian, unlike Kit, has not lost touch with the presumably inborn femininity that qual-ifies her to step back into the role the woman is supposed to play within the private sphere: she is so innately noble, she weeps the first time she witnesses an opera, despite the fact that she has never been exposed to this cultural form before (Edward explains to her that you either get it the first time or it will never "be part of your soul"); she is so innately domestic, she instinctively refers to the penthouse hotel room where she sleeps with her temporary employer as "home" and repeatedly draws his attention to the emotional life he represses and neglects. Her role, as the classic domes-tic woman, will be to soften and humanize his commercial experience; her power is in her feminine influence over the man whose agency will show its effects in the public sphere. He is afraid of heights, he is afraid of com-mitment, he is afraid of feeling, he is afraid of intimate connection: her feminine influence will inspire him to overcome these fears, and to "do the right thing" by the rival businessman he has contemplated destroying.

The "Pretty Woman's" power is in her prettiness, her ability to draw the look: she exists to be looked at, to be the object of the gaze that is

persistently, repeatedly framed as fixated on her body. Whether she is presented as a tramp or a lady, blonde-wigged and miniskirted or elegantly
fitted up in her own luxuriantly red-dyed hair and "obscenely" expensive
clothes, everyone on the street and in the hotel lobby always stares at her.
The goal in her transformation from prostitute to acceptable companion
for Edward is not that she would draw fewer stares in public, but that the
stares would shift from lecherous shock to lecherous approval. She would
be perfectly beautiful, he repeatedly tells her, if she would only stop fid-
geting; all she needs to do to be a real lady is to act like one in public as
she has already begun to do in private. Her reward for softening his masculine commercial impulses will be the climactic penultimate scene: he
overcomes his fear of heights and of commitment, climbs her balcony, and
"rescues her": and she, in turn, follows the logic of domestic ideology and
"rescues him right back" by accepting his apology for having suggested a
long-term financial arrangement that would have made her his prostitute
in perpetuity.[1] Now, we are to assume, she can be his wife instead. In
all her prettiness she can be an icon of the kind of feminine power some
first-wave Victorian feminists extolled, the model of femininity that post-
feminists are embracing, which second- and third-wave feminists have
endlessly (and, I think, definitively) analyzed as twentieth-century
women's subjugation.

   That's only a fraction of what I could say about the regressive gender
politics of this popular marriage-plot text (to be sure, many feminist commentators have said much more),[2] but let's call it enough. This standard
feminist reading assumes that the plot's motor is desire, its excitement primarily sexual. But what is odd about *Pretty Woman* as a marriage-plot
movie is the fact that the sex comes first, not last. The protagonists are
having sex—good sex, too, it's implied—from the beginning of their storyline; sexual consummation is the starting point, not the end point, of
their plot. In the representation of their relationship, this entails a curious
reversal of the order in which physical intimacy builds: they have intercourse first, kiss later. The excitement of the storyline, then, is not about
when orgasm will occur; orgasms are occurring throughout Vivian and
Edward's week together—they're a given, they're background noise, like
the rising operatic motif (perversely invoking *La Traviata*) that recurs in
the final scene. The orgasms just accompany the action. The excitement
this movie evokes comes from other developments in the heroine's life: the
access to limitless resources that results from her alliance to a wealthy
man; the opulence of the hotel penthouse, with its elaborate furniture,
stunning view of L.A., and swimming-pool-sized bathtub; the endless
supply of sumptuous food (he orders everything on the menu for her first

room-service breakfast—the table groans under pancakes, eggs, cereal, while she chooses that most elegant of yuppie breakfast items, a croissant; on their first evening out, her principal challenge is figuring out how to manage the table utensils that will convey the multicourse gourmet meal to her famously wide, smiling mouth); the lived fantasy of having carte blanche and personal "sucking up" service at a Rodeo Drive boutique— and especially of avenging the snub she had received at a rival boutique by flaunting the commissions the saleswomen there had lost by slighting her. All this is carefully set up to contrast with the squalor of Vivian's apartment building, the paucity of the prostitutes' meals (Kit uses a bartender's supply of citrus, olives, cherries, and cocktail onions as a "buffet"), and the shabbiness of the clothes she can afford (Vivian repairs the scuffs on her hip boots with magic marker). And there is the ancillary excitement of the possibility that, in marrying Vivian, Edward will change who she is: she will no longer be a struggling working woman risking disease, drug addiction, abuse, and death—all possibilities the movie invokes with its opening scene's police investigation of a strung-out prostitute's evident homicide—but a well-heeled wife; she will no longer be a trampy girl who gauchely places her body in inappropriate places (she is constantly sitting down on breakfast tables or department store display cases) and accidentally shoots escargot shells across elegant restaurants, but a well-behaved lady. Her identity, her very self will be transformed if he marries her. And, oh yes, of course, they'll have sex—but they've been doing that all along anyway. They've even kissed on the mouth, long before the movie's ending: the consummation of sexual desire is not what we're waiting for. But what are the affects this plot invokes?

As I watch, I experience interest/excitement ("eyebrows down, track, look, listen," [Sedgwick and Frank, *Silvan Tomkins Reader*, 74]); enjoyment ("smile, lips widened up and out," 74); and shame ("eyes down, head down," 74). The accelerated pulse and pleasure of the interest and enjoyment alternate with the mild nausea of the shame, depending on whether I am attending to the text's overt narrative or to my almost compulsively experienced ideological critique, both of the text and of my enjoyment. I can account for the mix in narratological terms: interest and enjoyment mark my face when I am responding to the intradiegetic level of the action, the exchanges among the characters; to the extent that I can participate at the extradiegetic level as a member of the film's intended audience, I feel the widening up and out of my lips, the absorbed track-look-listen signifying excitement. But at a metadiegetic level that opens up when I adopt the perverse strategy of self-conscious, self-consciously feminist close reading, my eyes lower, my head is down: shame sets in.

As I observe my own reactions, I cannot help but think of Elizabeth Bennet's feeling, in Jane Austen's *Pride and Prejudice,* on seeing Mr. Darcy's estate shortly after having refused his first offer of marriage: "To be mistress of Pemberley might be something!" Not to be mistress of Mr. Darcy, not specifically to get to have sanctioned sexual intercourse with him, but to be mistress of Pemberley. That something would be exactly what Vivian stands to gain by marrying Edward: access to economic resources and luxury, and a dramatic upwardly mobile change in social identity. If *Pretty Woman*'s marriage plot is not governed by the telos of sexual consummation, that doesn't mean it is not a classic marriage-plot text; what it does mean is that the affective shape of the marriage plot has always been about something other than (or at least something that is not identical to) sexual desire. Even Jane Austen won't let you forget this: witness Elizabeth's notorious reply to her sister's question about when she began loving Mr. Darcy: "I believe I must date it from my first seeing his beautiful grounds at Pemberley." Jane responds by entreating Elizabeth to "be serious," and it's easy to attribute Elizabeth's joke to the heroine's own self-conscious irony, or the double awareness Austen's texts always evince of the ways middle-class women's marital aspirations must combine sexual attraction with material security if they are to succeed under the model of companionate marriage. But *Pretty Woman* surprises me by showing how marriage-plot texts evince that double awareness even when they are not—like Austen novels—intentionally ironic, when their latent messages—as well as their manifest ones—are demonstrably both antiwoman and antifeminist.

I would not be surprised if Jane Bennet's response to Elizabeth's joke had been "for shame, Lizzie": indeed, given Austen's practice of rendering dialogue in free indirect discourse, it might as well be what Jane says when she asks her sister to be serious. For if being mistress of Pemberley "might be something," there is definitely something shameful in the baldly economic and material sources of excitement I have been describing, the flaunted middle-class feminine wish for more and better stuff. *Pretty Woman* shames me by alternating scenes of material plenitude with scenes that reinforce the commercial nature of the transaction between the two protagonists, just as Edward shames Vivian when he reminds her that "we both screw people for money."

At another level of the diegesis, however, *Pretty Woman* engages the lover of marriage plots in a more subtle kind of shaming, a persistent reminder that this narrative exists in a tradition of marriage plots, and that its pleasures are as formulaically induced as they are materialistic. The scene I have been discussing immediately precedes a brief quotation from the Audrey Hepburn–Cary Grant movie, *Charade,* the last moment of that film, in which Hepburn's lines make it clear that she is simultaneously accepting Cary Grant's marriage proposal and admitting that she does not know his real name, does not even know whether he is a government agent, a con man, or a thief—"I love you," she declares, "whoever you are." As the remote in Vivian's hand clicks off the TV, one of those metadiegetic moments occurs: evidently in spite of itself and its overt project, *Pretty Woman* reminds us that Audrey Hepburn—that other, earlier *gamine* with the improbably wide smile and the impossibly thin body—and Julia Roberts are functionally the same pretty woman, the same heroine in the same narrative tradition, where marriage is the only possible outcome despite the absurdity of the circumstances leading to it. It's a long and venerable tradition, a convention linking up such unlikely brides as Shakespeare's Beatrice, Brontë's Jane Eyre, and Eliot's Dorothea Brooke. To invoke Nancy Miller's classic characterization of eighteenth- and nineteenth-century British and French euphoric and dysphoric novels, the heroine could get married or she could die: for the feminocentric marriage plot, there is no other conceivable end. The glimpse at the screwball-comic resolution of *Charade* places the self-conscious close reader momentarily outside *Pretty Woman*'s diegesis, inside a critical space where the ironies of the marriage-plot convention come briefly and vividly into the foreground.

Another such metadiegetic moment comes at *Pretty Woman*'s end: rather than concluding with the romantic climbing of Vivan's balcony, the mutual rescue, the big kiss, the final scene pans back to show the couple standing in the midst of Vivian's squalid neighborhood. Along with the theme from *La Traviata,* the soundtrack picks up the refrain of the black man who had been walking the streets in the opening scene, declaiming: "This is Hollywood, Hollywood, where dreams come true. . . ." Yes, it's Hollywood: on the intradiegetic level, Hollywood is the town next door to Beverly Hills, the location of prostitution, drug addiction, poverty, and death; at the extradiegetic level of the film's evidently intended reader, Hollywood is the source of movies that confirm fairy-tale wishes for "happy endings"; and at the metadiegetic level of the perverse lover of marriage plots, the self-consciously feminist close reader, Hollywood is the perpetuator and reinforcer of the myth behind the marriage-plot formula and its affective impact on its audience. Eyes down, head lowered: shame at the predictability and the crassness of it all mixes with the smile of enjoyment; eyes down, head lowered, smiling—this is the posture of gendered feeling that Hollywood inscribes on the faces of effeminate viewers of "chick flicks," again and again, every time devotees of this genre read another marriage plot.

What this body-conscious reading strategy has to offer to the effeminate/feminist reader is the added aspect of surprise; eyebrows raised, eyes blinking, I am startled by those metadiegetic moments where the mainstream popular text points to the ricketiness of its own machinery (the predictability, the formulaicness of it all). It's physically impossible for a face to register the affects of shame—eyes lowered, head down—and surprise simultaneously: when my eyebrows go up and my eyes blink, the feeling of effeminate experience changes. For me the relief of the change offsets the discomfort of the ambivalence that inspires it.

CHAPTER FOUR

The Thrill and the Yawn: Antieffeminate Structures of Feeling in Serial Forms

"There is a male sort of loneliness that adheres in programming." At least, that's what Ellen Ullman (1996), an engineer writing about the way she and her colleagues use e-mail, believes. It's the loneliness, she explains, that prevailed among the boys she knew in her childhood who tried to ameliorate their own isolation not by socializing, in the sense of encountering other people in a common space, but by tinkering with CB radios and sending out messages; it's an ambivalent loneliness that moves the lonesome person to try to connect with others, but to mediate that attempted connection through a machine that imposes certain limits on the quality, the intensity, and the content of the relationships it brings into existence. That "male sort of loneliness" intrigues me as an example of a gendered feeling. Ullman admits to sharing that feeling (and, once I had read her essay, which I'll be talking about at the end of this chapter, I realized I share it, too), so I would question the use of "male" to modify the "loneliness"; I might call it a "masculine" loneliness, a function of gender rather than of sex, except that "masculine" already has too many competing denotations to be useful here. I will, therefore, call this an "antieffeminate" feeling, placing it into contrast with the affects resulting from the textual technologies of effeminacy I have discussed so far.

As distinct but parallel technologies of feeling, serial fiction and e-mail have a lot in common, especially in terms of gender. e-mail began as an overwhelmingly masculine medium, in the sense that the vast majority of the original e-mail users were persons in traditionally "male" occupations, though in recent years it has expanded far beyond the realms of engineers that Ullman describes. Serial novels published by trade presses, too, tend in the late twentieth century to address antieffeminate audiences. My question is, how does serial form—as it manifests itself in popular serial novels and in e-mail correspondence—give shape to the affective life of the antieffeminate reader's body? After outlining the ways that serial form operates generally to structure readers' feelings in Trollope's texts, I will turn to the feelings invoked by two specific instances of anti-effeminate serial, e-mail correspondence and serialized historical novels.

Narratives can be understood as devices for structuring what bodies do in time and space: not only do narratives offer representations of "virtual" time and space whose imaginary deployments leave real effects—in the form of feelings—on readers' bodies, narratives also take up "real" time in the lives of audiences who have to "make space" in their days for reading or for viewing. In its length, its repetitiousness, its management of suspense, and its resistance to closure, serial form exaggerates the typical narrative deployment of time and space, both virtual and real. The feelings that come with following a serial are the feelings associated with all narratives, only "more so": serials structure feelings that are more predictable, more familiar, more formulaic, and—for the aficionado of any particular series—more intense.

In a recent study of the interactions between serial texts and their audiences over the past century and a half, Jennifer Hayward (1997) enumerates elements that all serials share: "These include refusal of closure; intertwined subplots; large casts of characters (incorporating a diverse range of age, gender, class, and increasingly, race representation to attract a similarly diverse audience); interaction with current political, social, or cultural issues; dependence on profit; and acknowledgement of audience response (this has become increasingly explicit, even institutionalized within the form, over time)" (3). Hayward points to the formal features serials have in common, including "intertwined subplots . . . dramatic plot reversals . . . [and] distinctive (and much derided) narrative tropes: sudden returns from the dead, doubles, long-lost relatives, marginal or grotesque characters, fatal illness, dramatic accidents, romantic triangles, grim secrets, dramatic character transformations" (4).[1] She emphasizes, however, that what makes serials distinct are not these thematic elements, present in many other genres, but their combination with "the unique reading practices and interpretative tactics developed by audiences, practices that include collaborative, active reading; interpretation; prediction; occasional rewriting or creation of new subplots; attempts to influence textual production; and, increasingly often, a degree of success in those attempts" (4). Hayward notes that serial forms have acquired increasingly strongly gendered connotations in the modern and postmodern periods; building on her model of serial form, this chapter will investigate the affective implications of the gendering of serial fiction.

Whereas the audience for, say, Anthony Trollope's serial novels emerges from advertisements and from Trollope's texts as comprising masculine and feminine readers alike, serial texts of the late twentieth century tend to be much more rigidly gendered. If soap opera addresses a distinctly effeminate audience, serialized novels have taken an antieffeminate turn in their address. After a detailed consideration of Trollope's serial form, I will take Patrick O'Brian's serialized novels as a case in point to consider how twentieth-century serial fiction works to structure gendered affect for its antieffeminate readers.

Self-Conscious Serial Forms

Since its earliest emergence in part-issue novels and periodicals of the 1830s, serial narrative has increased in popularity in British and U.S. culture over the past 150 years. From prose fiction to radio, comics, film, and television, the cultural shift to mass media has made for a popular cultural milieu that is especially suited to the serial, which has been defined as "a continuing story over an extended time with enforced interruptions" (Hughes and Lund 1991, 2). The comic strip, the radio drama, the Hollywood film with sequels, the television series, even the broadcast advertisement: each is a narrative genre with "enforced interruptions" built in, and each has adapted serial form for the outlines of its continuing stories. Though some serial forms flourished throughout the twentieth century—notably the radio and television soap opera—other genres such as televised situation comedies and commercials only began incorporating serial elements in the 1980s. Before *Cosby* and *Roseanne,* the "situations" in situation comedies remained comparatively static, in order to maintain the formulas on which the comedy was based.[2] It was risky for *Cheers* in the 1980s to develop the highly touted sexual tension between Sam Malone and Diane Chambers into a consummated relationship that was to flourish and eventually fail, offering Shelley Long the unusual primetime opportunity of leaving the show without causing its demise; by the time *Friends* had become the most popular sitcom in the mid-1990s, the continuing story of the on-again-off-again romance between two of the six protagonists, Ross and Rachel, had become the main feature of the show's marketing campaign and the focus of its stories. The changes in casting, setting, and plot circumstances that accompany serial form became ordinary in 1990s evening television programs, in a way that would have been utterly foreign to primetime TV in the 1960s.

The history of *Star Trek* tracks with the rise of serial form in recent decades: whereas the original, 1960s series was highly episodic in its structure, its 1980s successor, *Star Trek: The Next Generation,* developed a continuing story line, making occasional references to the "backstory" provided by the first series. The more recent incarnations, *Star Trek: Voyager* and especially *Deep Space Nine,* present elaborate histories of a virtual future, politically and technologically consistent with each other and with the narratives developed in the first two series. Every episode has its own unified action (with a beginning, or exposition; a middle, or complications; and an end, or denouement), but each action in these later series plays a part in the continuing story of the whole.

In the latest versions of *Star Trek,* such science-fiction conventions as time travel—combined with new "real-world" technologies for digitally altering video images—lend themselves well to self-consciousness about how serial form works. When *Deep Space Nine* aired a special episode resurrecting some footage from an episode of the first *Star Trek* series, "The Trouble with Tribbles," the complications and delights of serial form came vividly into the foreground, as the 1990s actors stepped into scenes from the 1960s episode that are part of the fictitious history behind the *Deep Space Nine* narrative, and that have, for that matter, become part of the American popular-cultural collective memory.[3] When Captain Sisko and Engineering Chief O'Brian encounter Captain Kirk and Mr. Spock in a passageway on the original *Enterprise,* the layers of resonance for the long-term *Star Trek* fan reach back over thirty years: Kirk and Spock, oblivious to the intruders from the future (who are, from their perspective within the present diegesis, just two more anonymous *Enterprise* crew members, and who were, after all, not even present on the scene when it was first shot for the original "Trouble with Tribbles" episode), are historic heroes to Sisko and O'Brian, who gaze at them with an air of celebrity worship that mirrors the *Star Trek* audience's affectionate reverence for these two originary heroes and for William Shatner and Leonard Nimoy, the actors who have played Kirk and Spock off and on throughout the television and movie versions of the *Star Trek* series for three decades. The scene presents an iconic moment of the intertextual complications inherent in serial form: simultaneously, the present audience responds to the personas of Shatner and Nimoy, as they looked in the 1960s and as the audience knows they have come to look in the 1990s; to the characters of Kirk and Spock in the original episode and to the meanings those characters have come to hold within the fictitious histories behind the later series; to the current heroes, Sisko and O'Brian, in their present situation of time travel; and to Sisko's and O'Brian's appreciation of the "history" and the "heroes" they are witnessing. The manipulation of video images made possible by computer technology enables a literalization of the way past and present narrative details always intertwine in serial form.

Self-consciousness about seriality has led to popular-cultural texts that exploit serial form with postmodern insouciance. The primetime melodrama *Dallas* broke historic ground in the mid-1980s with its notorious "Pam's dream" episode, in which the audience learned that all the plots and subplots of the previous season (in which, among other important events, Bobby Ewing, Pam's husband, had died) were only a dream Pam had been having while Bobby, not at all dead, had been taking a shower. *Roseanne*'s 1997 final episode employed a similar strategy, claiming that the series's last year—and indeed an unspecified amount of its earlier diegesis, too—had been a novel Roseanne wrote in order to deal with her grief over losing her husband, Dan, to the heart attack he had suffered in the previous season. Both series appeared to be trying, as if in afterthought, to rectify story developments that viewers had found problematic, such as the loss of Patrick Duffy's popular character Bobby from *Dallas* or the uncharacteristic plot developments of *Roseanne*'s last year, including the Connors's winning the lottery and Dan's having an extramarital affair. In both series, employing the "it was only a dream/fiction" strategy wiped out a considerable accumulation of backstory in the series, requiring viewers to reconsider the meaning of present narrative events in terms of the new closure. For instance, Roseanne's voice-over at the end of the final episode explains that after Dan died from the heart attack, she felt so angry and betrayed by his leaving her it was as if he had had an affair; hence she had written his imagined affair, but not his death, into her novel. The strategy presents fewer problems for the viewer at the end of a series, as in *Roseanne,* than when it happens midstream, as in *Dallas.* Watching *Dallas* in the season after Pam's dream presented a bizarrely challenging task for long-term viewers, as they were required in interpreting each new scene to recall whether the relevant details of backstory "happened" during the year that was wiped out (and hence "never really happened") or sometime during the decade before that year. Ultimately, the narrative of *Dallas* had to dissolve, as the long-term story became impossible for viewers to reconstruct.

The introduction of "Pam's dream" into the serial narrative of *Dallas* represented a flippancy toward the genre's basic conventions that is seldom present in popular-culture serials, even when they begin as parodies of the form. Both *Mary Hartman, Mary Hartman* and *Soap,* two TV sitoms initially presented as spoofs of soap opera, eventually developed elaborate serial plots that consistently followed all the genre's conventions while simultaneously holding them up for ridicule. Similarly, the Taster's Choice ad campaign that developed a story of romance between an exaggeratedly arch and sophisticated heterosexual pair of neighbors very carefully traced out, over the course of two years of broadcasts and half a dozen separate commercials, their initial flirtation, their jealous curiosity about each other's social lives, the woman's present relations with her ex-husband and adult son, and the implicit consummation of their interest in each other when they meet up in the final episode, a commercial set in Paris.[4] Exploiting all the serial conventions of formulaic relationships, repetition with variation, and suspended action, these ads presented some competition for the programs they supported, in terms of audience interest. The Taster's Choice campaign culminated in a contest that addressed readers of paperback romance, challenging them to write a suitable ending for the series in order to qualify for a prize (it was, I believe, a trip to Paris). I think, though, that the marketers responsible for that campaign mistook their genre. If romance novels require an ending, serial narratives actively resist coming to closure: formally speaking, the Taster's Choice series could have continued indefinitely, in emulation of the serials it both spoofed and imitated so well. Effeminate or not, the serial audience isn't interested in the story's end; for them, resolutions are always provisional, and closure is only temporary. The ambivalent agitation that comes with a sense of open-endedness, of continued possibility, and of the contingency of events is part of what it feels like to follow a serial over the long term. I call it ambivalent because that agitation seems paradoxically to be accompanied by a soothing effect that readers call "calming" or even "boring," an effect I locate—along with the excitement of agitation—in the serial form itself.

Reading the (Boring) Victorian Serial

Anthony Trollope's two six-novel series, each made up of fictions published in parts, are my models for the ways Victorian serial fiction worked to structure readers' feelings. I want to describe what reading a Trollope serial feels like, or might have felt like, for a dedicated modern or Victorian Trollope fan. While many of my observations about reading Trollope are extrapolations from Trollope's textual practices or indeed from my own responses, I also consult the reactions of actual readers, friends and colleagues who have reported their feelings in conversation or in print. For instance, Paula Marantz Cohen, in *The Daughter as Reader* (1996), offers a vivid account of the emotional effect of reading Trollope, which she recommends in an essay called "RX for Premature Labor." Telling the story of the extreme physical and emotional distress she experienced when her second child appeared to be being born not quite two-thirds of the way through her pregnancy, Cohen reports that only two remedies effectively relieved her anxiety during her time in the hospital: a shot of morphine, and the serial novels of Trollope. Reading Trollope,

Cohen explains, had a calming effect that could not be matched by contemporary popular novels, television, or magazines: to escape her nervous preoccupation with her premature contractions, she says, "I needed to be embraced by an all-encompassing alternative reality, and the magazines, like the TV game shows and sitcoms that I tried to watch, were little patchwork pieces. They did not define a world and hence had no ability to fasten me to them" (81). Many patients in her situation would turn from the game shows and sitcoms to soap operas, but Cohen does not even mention that possibility. Herself a professional critic of nineteenth-century novels who had felt little interest in Trollope before her hospitalization, Cohen says now that her baby is safely delivered, "I no longer need Trollope. But I have developed a sentimental attachment to the idea of him and have sought to find specific reasons for the calming effect he had on me" (83). Most of Cohen's reasons strike me as somewhat elitist or canonical academic arguments for avoiding Trollope in any circumstances other than the kind of emergency she describes: he is, she says, "the consummate *daydreamer*," whereas "great writers are not principally daydreamers" (84).

Cohen's account of the calming effect of Trollope's fiction seems to me to belittle the experience of reading Trollope's serials by categorizing the activity literally as escapist. She locates the source of her feelings in the thematic material of Trollope's stories, but I think the calming effect of Trollope is more directly attributable to the form of his fiction than to its content. Cohen glances at this possibility when she writes that, reading Trollope, "one is carried on the current of plot, lulled by the assurance that one's expectations about people and events will be fulfilled in due time" (86). That assurance comes from the conventions of serial form, the structure that made it possible for this particular reader to reconfigure her physical experience of affect in a period of intense nervous crisis. Cohen says reading Trollope made her feel calm; D. A. Miller—about whom I will have more to say in the next section—says it makes him feel bored. Calm and boredom: among those states we might call "feelings," these two are remarkable for being characterized by a *lack* of affect; they are the feelings that negate feeling. My purpose in investigating Trollope's serial form is to find the confluence of readerly feelings that leads to this evident negation of affect, a state of (non)feeling our culture marks as the opposite of effeminacy.

From a readerly perspective, Trollope's novels were originally published in three different serial modes: part-issue, publication in periodicals, and series of novels. Those novels appearing in "part-issue" first came out in paperback monthly parts, appearing in complete hardbound editions once the last part had been published; those others appearing in periodicals came out weekly, fortnightly, or monthly in magazines containing advertisements, articles, reviews, and other fictions. Both of these two modes of publication enforced regularly timed gaps in the original audience's reception of the novel's plot; no matter how quickly a reader might take in the two or four chapters of a monthly part, serial publication dictated a pause between each part, as the audience waited for the next number to be distributed. According to Trollope's *Autobiography*, novels appearing serially in magazines were considered a thrifty alternative to those whose parts appeared independently. Trollope seems to have favored the mode of part issue, and—when he could—he continued in that mode into and beyond the 1860s, when it was no longer the common practice Dickens and Thackeray had made it earlier in the century.[5] (*Can You Forgive Her?* 1864–65 and *The Prime Minister*, 1875–76, for example, both appeared in monthly part-issues, though the three intervening volumes in the Palliser series came out in various periodicals, *St. Paul's Magazine*, the *Fortnightly Review*, and the *Graphic*, respectively.) Hence the appearance and immediate context of parts in a series would vary, in contrast to contemporary soap operas, which can appear daily for decades in the same time slots on the same television networks. Pecuniary considerations aside, the appearance of serialized fiction in periodical reviews is a scholarly and pedagogical boon, since it makes the varying intertextual context of a novel so manifestly available, but it only makes more obvious a fact that is always true of serial fictions published in either of these two modes: the first readings of those novels were inevitably interrupted, interspersed with readings of other fictional and nonfictional texts. In both modes, part-issue and periodicals, readers might enter the serialized novel in mid-action, and—if they were to be caught up by the narrative—those latecomers would need access to a plot already in progress. At any given moment in the serialized text, the narrator is speaking to a range of possible audiences, from the devoted readers who remember every detail from parts that were published weeks, months, and even years earlier, to those whose first entry into the novel is the present installment.

In the third serial mode—novels published in parts that are themselves parts of longer series, such as the Palliser and the Barsetshire novels—this variety of possible audiences becomes even greater. For any given number, any four-chapter segment of a novel, the audience might or might not know the details of thousands of pages of "backstory." While the gaps in reading time between the parts of each novel proceeded with a predictable regularity, typically a month at a time, the gaps between novels in a series were much less clearly established. The Barsetshire Chronicles appeared over a period of twelve years, the first three novels being published within a three-year period, and the next three coming out at three-year intervals thereafter. The Palliser series took sixteen years to unfold, with gaps as short as one year but also as long as four and five years between the volumes. The Victorian readers of Trollope's series, then, might follow a series for as many years as do many contemporary fans of television soap operas, but their affective experience of the story's momentum and its pauses—predictable enough while any one novel was being serialized— would proceed irregularly over the long term.

While these logistical considerations are no longer directly relevant to the reader of Trollope—who can, after all, go into any Barnes and Noble and buy all six novels in either series, or even order them all from Books on Tape (both are available, the Barsetshire Chronicles on ninety-six cassettes, and the Palliser novels on one hundred and eleven) and read them through just as steadily as he or she can manage to—the vicissitudes of serial composition and serial reception make their marks on the form of Trollope's text and, I would argue, on the feelings it invokes in the contemporary reader. For, even when they are published in volumes, Trollope's novels produce and reproduce the conventional moves of serial form. Those conventions include five typical features that set serial novels apart from other long, realistic narrative fictions: (1) Serials depend on systematically included *recapitulations* of past events that have already been either dramatized or narrated in the text, passages that repeat narrative details the persistent reader already knows, but that the late-arriving reader needs to have in order to put together the pieces of the subsequent story. Predictably, the further advanced the narrative, the more frequent the recapitulations, so that later installments of a serialized novel include more recaps than earlier parts do; (2) Serial plots are built upon *formulaic situations* familiar to the aficionado of the genre (in this case, serialized realist fiction), enabling the late-arriving reader to draw as much on formula as on recapitulations to enter the flow of the story line, and giving the long-term reader the grounds for guessing what will happen next; (3) Serials' plot formulas depend more than other realistic genres on *coincidence*, in order to reintroduce characters who have receded from the foreground of the narrative; (4) Serialized fiction specializes in setting up *readerly expectations*, then meeting or thwarting them. Indeed, all Victorian and modern narrative fiction does this, but serial fiction emphasizes this aspect of narrative structure by manipulating the gaps between a story's installments; (5) Serial fiction also conventionally displays a stronger *resistance to closure* even than has already been identified in nineteenth-century fictions more generally. This keeping the story open, keeping it moving forward, is a pattern that gets established for obvious reasons at the ends of individual installments within each novel, but it also operates in the conclusions of entire novels, especially those that are parts of longer series.

D. A. Miller (1981) has very astutely remarked that "if closure does not carry much conviction in Trollope, it doesn't need to, [because] the social security that traditional closure means to establish has been displaced into the tensions, differences, and disequilibriums that engender or motivate the narrative processes themselves" (123). In other words, the social order of the world Trollope represents is so stable in the first place, it hardly requires narrative closure to reestablish its stability; the very conflicts that structure Trollope's plots hold the social order in stasis. In Miller's reading this is a matter of thematics, but I would argue that the thematic effect emerges from the serial form itself. I think it's very interesting that Miller, one of the most form-sensitive of all narrative critics, doesn't even mention seriality in his close analysis of the narrative movement of *Barchester Towers*. Nor does he mention it in his vivid afterword on what it *feels* like to read Trollope: as he so memorably puts it, "When I read Trollope, it is all I can do not to be bored" (145).

Boredom is built into the serial form. It is a product of the familiarity, the formulaic nature, the predictability, and especially the repetitiveness of Trollope's texts. Miller understands his boredom at reading Trollope's novels—and indeed, Trollope's evident boredom in writing them—as the other side of horrified fascination, a defense against the violent erasure of individual subjectivity implied by Trollope's social order. "Far from the simple reflex-response to banality, boredom hysterically converts into yawning affectlessness what would otherwise be outright panic" (145). Seductive as I find this psychoanalytic reading to be, I want to consider the possibility that boredom is not "affectlessness," but is itself a state of feeling, a physical response to the inexorable repetitiousness of Trollope's serial form.[6] Like Miller, I don't think that Trollope's text is "simply" boring: why else would we keep reading it? I think the boredom is part of a complex set of fascinatingly conflicting feelings built in to the serial form, serving as a complementary counterbalance to the heightened sense of suspense and tension that automatically come with the gaps between installments.

Consider what it feels like to follow a serial story: for the initiated reader, the devotee who knows not just the genre but the text in question from its first installment, there's the affective engagement that comes with absorption in a fiction's forward motion; then there's a suspension of that engagement during the pause enforced by the gap between parts, a pause characterized by the feelings of tension associated with suspense ("What will happen next?") and of that other very pleasurable feeling—the self-satisfaction and security of feeling oneself to be an "insider" or of being one "in the know," I suppose—inspired by formula-based speculation ("I'll bet I can guess what will happen next"). Then with the next install-ment comes the pleasure of the resumed narrative flow, then reengage-ment mixed with an inevitable amount of boredom at the repetitions that are offered for the less well-informed reader. For the reader who joins a serial in progress, there's at first a degree of emotional detachment in entering a narrative whose details are as yet remote or incoherent, then the feeling of being caught into engagement (at least partly through those same repetitions that are so boring to the initiated reader), then that same mixture of suspense and speculation during the pauses that the devotee experiences, then the same reengagement mixed with tedium, for now the newly arrived reader is a devotee, too.

The activity of reading serially follows a predictable sequence, then, of alternating and oscillating feelings. While bored, the devoted readers are also engaged; while suspended passively between installments, they are also actively speculating about outcomes; while propelled forward by the story's momentum toward developing those outcomes, they are invested in the text's keeping the conflicts unresolved, keeping the installments or the series going indefinitely. One of the strongest pulls of serial fiction is the obscure hope that this alternation of feelings might—as indeed day-time soap operas sometimes do—go on literally for a lifetime; a series of novels like the Pallisers, weighing in at around 4,375 pages in modern editions, seems almost to hold out that promise. This alternation of engagement with tedium and of suspense with speculation adds up to a profound ambivalence that leaves its marking on the reader's affective life, creating a pattern over the long term that I think of as performative: by putting the reader's body through a repeated series of feelings, reading serially constitutes a definable aspect of gendered, bourgeois subjectivity. And, as an insight of Hayward's (1997) makes clear, this particular set of feelings would be specific to the bourgeoisie and working class, but not to upper-class readers in the Victorian period: "Since the most expensive texts were still three-volume novels, available only to those who could afford either their purchase or a circulating-library subscription, less afflu-ent readers were forced to consume Dickens installments by cheap but anxiety-producing installment. Even library membership was economi-cally circumscribed; only the rich could afford a three-volume ticket, while less well off subscribers were restricted to a single volume at a time and thus could not guarantee their ability to finish a novel. That middle- and upper-class readers sometimes chose to evade the close intersection of part-issue fiction and everyday life, with the anxiety this intersection produced, can be seen in the journals and diaries some readers have left us" (37). In reading practice as in other economically influenced things, class status and anxiety level are thus directly correlated.

The feelings involved in reading serially are always literally mixed, for reading serially is as wickedly ironic as it is ambivalent. Whenever a serial installment performs a recapitulation of previously narrated information, the text addresses audiences with very different needs: the new reader who simply lacks the information, and the persistent readers who already know the details (though they may indeed have forgotten) and who risk boredom every time they encounter a recapitulation. Trollope's texts—very like the daytime soap opera—address this situation by adding ironic valences to repeated material, giving the devoted reader an extra *frisson* of humorous recognition to offset the tedium of the repeated detail. This plays itself out as repetition with variation, a characteristic feature of Trollope's style, even at the level of the sentence.[7] Consider a classically Trollopian example, part of the description of Everett Wharton in *The Prime Minister* (p. 14): "It cannot be said of him that he did much thinking for himself;—but he thought that he thought." For repetition with variation, this seems to me comparable to Gertrude Stein's famous remark about Oakland, California, that "There is no there there." In Trollope's sentence as in Stein's, a word is repeated three times, and yet the sentence contains no redundancy. In the example from Trollope, the word "think" appears in two different forms, the gerund "thinking" and the past-tense "thought," and it occurs three times in just two lines. The glory of this sentence is its dogged insistence on saying three different things with the same word, for each time the word carries a somewhat different force: "thinking for himself" would be one activity, in this case one that Everett cannot achieve; but "he thought" says there's another activity he *can* achieve, that is, conceiving a false idea about himself. The third usage, "that he thought," appears merely to repeat the past-tense form of the second use of the word, but in its sense it actually harks back to the first usage ("thinking for himself")—the same word comes back in this brief sentence again and then again but each time with a humorously inflected difference. I offer this sentence as an extreme example of how the repetitiveness of Trollope's prose works itself out on the sentence level, but I am arguing that each installment of Trollope's serial novels does the same thing with repeating elements of the story as this sentence does with variations on the word "think."

Of course, repetitiveness on the level of style and of structure might just be further evidence for Miller's contention that "Trollope always seems a little bored himself" (145); therefore I looked for signs of any purposefulness in the repetitions that made their way into the manuscript of one of Trollope's freestanding serial novels, *The Belton Estate.* Trollope's editorial revisions suggest that, from the author's perspective, such repetitions serve a purpose when they do occur: Trollope evidently preferred not to repeat a word in a sentence or in near proximity if he could avoid it. To avoid boring my own reader with what might be received as tedious detail, I offer just one typical example, though the manuscript provides many more: "They told him that his family could be traced back to very early days,—before the Plantagenets, as he believed, though on this point of the subject he was very hazy in his [here the MS cancels "ideas," substituting "information"],—and he liked the *idea* of being the man by whom the family should be reconstructed in its glory" (MS no. 10, chap. 20, p. 29).[8] I cite this editorial practice, not so much as evidence of authorial intention (for even if that were determinable, what relevance would it have to the question of serial reading?), but rather as traces of the machinery of repetition working itself out in serial form. For there is, of course, something wondrously mechanical about Trollope's composing process, a mechanics that renders the serial form even that much more visible when you analyze the plot structure of each of the parts.

Looking at the manuscript of *The Belton Estate,* I was powerfully struck by what every Trollope scholar of course knows, but what you come to realize more viscerally when you hold Trollope's holograph in your hand: the regularity of the production, the signs of the routine of daily and fortnightly writing, are so palpable as to be almost overwhelming. Every installment of this novel contains two chapters and is *exactly* forty handwritten pages long. Trollope's pages are twenty-five to twenty-seven lines long; a line contains about ten words. Some installments of *The Belton Estate* end in the upper third or half of page 40, some go to the bottom of the page, but the variation in length among the parts is never more than about two hundred words. The chapters are roughly twenty manuscript pages long: at the beginning (parts 1 and 2) and at the end (part 16) the first of the two chapters in the number is a little longer (twenty-four or twenty-five pages); in three sections near the middle (parts 7, 10, 11) the first chapter is a couple of pages shorter (eighteen, sixteen, and sixteen pages respectively), giving more space to the second. All the other numbers begin with a chapter that is twenty, twenty-one, or twenty-two pages long, and end exactly on page 40. In two cases (chapters 8 and 11) Trollope squeezed three lines into the margin of the last page of the first chapter in a number. Aside from those six lines, there's no visible cutting to shorten the length, no interpolations to increase it: the text just came out in this preternaturally regular way. The penmanship does deteriorate at the end of numbers, and most especially at the end of the very last chapter: Trollope's famous fatigue and hurry toward the end of installments—so notoriously addressed by the narrator of *Barchester Towers*—is clearly in evidence.

The astonishing machine that produced these texts, the Trollope of the manuscript, looks tired and a little rushed to me, true, but not bored, exactly. Indeed, Trollope advised aspiring novelists to "beware of creating tedium," adding that he knew "no guard against this so likely to be effective as the feeling of the writer himself" (*Autobiography* 241). I looked at the passages of recapitulation in *The Belton Estate* for signs that repetitions at the level of plot were as seemingly purposeful as those that occur in Trollope's sentences, and I was not altogether disappointed. Predictably, given their function for the late-arriving reader, recapitulations occur much more frequently and at greater length in the second half of the novel than they do in the first. Out of a total of sixteen installments, seven of the last eight contain recapitulative passages, and if we can deduce anything from the absence of corrections or revisions in Trollope's manuscript, these repetitions of plot elements must have been anticipated in his working notes, for they are seldom revised. Once I caught the author reminding himself that Lady Aylmer had only dictated an insulting letter Captain Aylmer sends to his fiancée, Clara, correcting an assertion that Lady Aylmer herself had written the letter: "The letter which [MS cancels "Lady," substitutes "Captain"] Aylmer had written to her about Mrs. Askerton will perhaps be remembered, and Clara's answer to that letter" (p. 343 Oxford; MS no. 13, chap. 26, p. 28). Judging by the intensity of the ink in the revision, it looks to me as if Trollope caught his error before reaching the end of that manuscript page. In the clearest example of intentional recapitulation I found, however, the manuscript reveals the author slowing down a passage of free indirect discourse where the heroine surveys her recent past, adding details that are less important for the conclusions Clara must draw than for the comprehension of the reader who has joined the serial late. Here, the narrator says, "Clara thought of all the events which had occurred to her since the last summer,—of their agony of grief at the catastrophe which had closed her brother's life, of—" At this point, the narrator was going on to speak of "the two offers of marriage she had received," but the writer cancels it before proceeding to the next line of text, in order to add two intervening plot details: "her aunt's death first and then of her father's following so close upon the other, and of the two offers of marriage made to her,—as to which she was now aware that she had accepted the wrong man and rejected the wrong man"[9] (no. 14, chap. 28, p. 31). The offers of marriage actually precede the deaths of the father and the aunt in the plot, but Clara's awareness of her mistake only becomes clear in the aftermath of the two deaths. For the reader of this passage in number 14 who had missed numbers 5 through 9 where the two deaths occurred, the brief repetitions bring up the exceptionally trying circumstances under which Clara had come to repent her choice. For the reader who knows these details perfectly well, as they have been mentioned dozens of times by the narrator and by the characters since their occurrence, the repetition is just tedious, and can be offset only by the implication that Clara, realizing her mistake, will continue to delay her marriage to Captain Aylmer and keep the conditions of narratability open indefinitely.

If Trollope's writing the repetitious recapitulations is a sign of narratorial activity rather than authorial boredom, what is the audience's experience in reading them? As I have said, it is an experience of mixed feelings, a delicate balance between the sleepiness induced by tedium, the internal chuckle aroused by irony, and the excitement of anticipating what's next. I am well aware that calling it complex doesn't make it interesting, as Miller (1981) has so pointedly remarked of Trollope's mode of characterization: "For what does the well-advertised complexity of his characters come to if not the simple effect, almost gimmicky in its insistence, of showing that they have 'mixed motives'?" (124). The serial structure of Trollope's plots is a gimmick, too, producing readers whose feelings are as mixed as his characters' motives. But the fact that it is a gimmick makes it all the more valuable for my purposes, in that it places this emotional patterning in such clear relief against the background of these enormously long and detailed narrative texts.

These are, to be sure, texts that occupy substantial amounts of their fans' "real time." As I have mentioned, each Trollope novel's original serialization would take many months to play out, and the entire series could continue for years. For the first audience of a serial, that long-term reading experience is continually interrupted by enforced pauses, as the novel's installments intermittently appear. While the gaps in reading time between the parts of each novel would proceed with a predictable regularity, typically a month or two weeks at a time, the gaps between novels in a series were much less regularly timed. As long as a series continued, readers could maintain a sense that the story was "not over," an open-ended promise of more to come, that would extend for more than a decade of a devoted reader's life. The appearance of a new two- or four-chapter segment in a periodical or in a part-issue pamphlet would mean the necessity of dedicating a stretch of time within that two-week or month-long period, to "keep up" with the story. The investment of time would pay off emotionally in the long run, that is, in the long-running satisfaction of the curiosity to know "what next? what next?" Publication in parts meant this question would occupy the committed reader's imagination between installments of a single novel; publication as a series meant the question could bridge the time that elapsed between the volumes within that series, as well.

The open-endedness of serial form, the necessity to resist closure and to keep the story going, even when matters seem to have been at least provisionally resolved in a previous volume's conclusion, has an effect on the form's management of "virtual time," or the time frame within the diegesis. This is particularly noticeable in Trollope's novels because they seem to follow the conventional dictates of the marriage plot: the amount of virtual time that is worth narrating, in any given novel, is the amount of time it takes for the various eligible characters to pair up and reach agreements with their families about their marital futures. The Palliser and Barsetshire novels usually follow a predictable formula: a young couple is attracted to each other, but faces impediments in the objection of one or more of their parents to what the older generation regards as a socially unsuitable match. Almost invariably this formula resolves itself in a happy marriage between the young couple (the miserable mistake Emily Wharton makes in marrying Ferdinand Lopez despite her father's objections forms a notable exception: not coincidentally, the marriage happens very early in *The Prime Minister*, giving Emily plenty of narrative time to become a widow and remarry, choosing the man of her father's choice at the novel's end). Sometimes, though, the conflict takes place not between ardent young persons and their reluctant parents, but within the desires of a young protagonist him- or herself; when this happens—as in *Phineas Finn*, where the hero falls in love no fewer than three times before finally marrying his first object of desire, or in *The Small House at Allington*, where Lily Dale becomes one of the very few virginal Victorian heroines to be unable to overcome an unfortunate first attachment, remaining single at the novel's end—the continuing series allows each volume's ostensible closure to become only tentative. Though Phineas marries at the end of his first volume, his young bride is dead before *Phineas Redux* begins, so his marriage plot starts over; Lily Dale, still unmarried to the faithful Johnny Eames at the beginning of *The Last Chronicle of Barset*, spends another volume resisting his importunities and—astoundingly enough, given her status as Victorian heroine—continues to remain single at the series's end. Marriage lends the conventional closure to the comic genre that would appear to be Trollope's métier, but marriage in serial novels—

as in daytime soap operas—is not at all a permanent condition. The ongoing serial form allows for an open-endedness of diegetic time that has profound effects on the characters' situations; insofar as those situations stir up responses, leaving their affective marks on readers who care about the characters' plights, this serial management of virtual time structures the reader's feelings. The trajectory of the marriage plot always moves forward, but in serial form, that forward movement seems never to stop—like those little "perpetual motion machines" that require just one push to rock back and forth on people's desks, seemingly forever—never coming fully to rest. The feelings of a serial's aficionado take their shape from that endless, intermittent motion.

Reading always takes place in "real space," where the reader's body sits, with eyes seeing or ears hearing a text. Serial reading (as opposed to television viewing) is more likely today than in Victorian times to put the reader in a lonesome space. The latest installment of a Trollope novel would have been a good candidate for reading aloud to the family in Victorian households that used this form of entertainment, though many middle-class Victorians would also read to themselves;[10] today, however, the serial reader is much more likely to read silently or to listen, with headphones or on the automobile cassette player, to a Books on Tape rendition of the series, all alone. (You need only consider how comparatively empty the car pool lanes are on freeways in large U.S. cities, to realize how many solitary drivers are whiling away the hours they spend in the other lanes' traffic jams.) Though serial reading might place the solitary reader (then or now) literally in an isolated space, serial fiction creates virtual spaces both inside and outside the diegesis that are locations for connection and contact with others. Outside the text, serial fiction creates a community of readers, all those other fans who "turn each other on" to favorite series, who exchange books as gifts and loans, who meet one-on-one or in groups, in person or online, on the World Wide Web or over E-mail, to talk about their predictions for and reactions to the fiction. And the virtual space within the fiction is the community that draws those readers together. Both Barsetshire and the Pallisers' "London" become stable, mappable places in Trollope's text, places readers can return to for contact with familiar characters who come and go according to more or less predictable formulas of plot development and coincidence. In Trollope's series, just as in daytime soap opera, the places are stable, the casts of characters variable. A favorite character might recede from the foreground of the story temporarily or even forever; the reader can never be sure whom the story will feature. But where the story happens is never at issue: in terms of virtual space, the habitual reader of Trollope serials is always at home.

Antieffeminate Affect

The aficionado of a Trollopian serial, then, would be subject to a certain set of affective conditions that would predictably accompany the reading experience. The lonesome feeling of silent reading would be offset by the communal feeling of familiarity serials breed, both inside and outside the fictions; the feeling of forward motion that accompanies the comic marriage plot would keep moving ahead indefinitely, never reaching a settled closure; the feeling of suspense would be more or less indefinitely maintained, as the story never reaches a definitive end. For the Victorian period, the feelings I am identifying did not carry connotations of gender, as Trollope's novels were neither directed to nor received by a specifically masculine or feminine audience.

Who were the readers that Victorian serials invoked? Hayward (1997) reports that "We know from contemporary journals and letters, as well as from reviews and sheer volume of sales, that both men and women read Dickens in apparently equal numbers" (19). Indeed the advertisements published with the serial segments of novels by Dickens and Trollope suggest that they were marketed to a mixed-gender, middle-class audience including men and women of various degrees of prosperity (those who would make decisions about which kitchen matches, stomach remedies, or tea to buy for a household, as well as those who would purchase bedsteads, camp furniture, men's clothing, eyeglasses, and insurance; those who consumed elaborate and expensive hunting equipment, and those who bought artificial nipples for baby bottles). Some of the ads in the part issues of *The Last Chronicle of Barset,* for example, are explicitly addressed to women, some to men: the audience implied by the thirty or forty ads encasing each issue of a part-issue novel includes masculine and feminine subjects, all implicitly anxious about upward mobility, social prominence, myopia, and dyspepsia. Each advertisement directly addresses a male or female purchaser, but as a whole the "Advertiser" (as the introductory section of each issue of serialized novels was called) assumes a readership of mixed gender.

Twentieth-century reversions to serial form are much more specifically gendered: daytime soap operas (with their ads for disposable diapers and baby formula, vaginal-yeast-infection treatments and tampons, cake mixes, laundry detergents, and other commodities for producing and cleaning up the detritus of the body's daily existence) are marketed to women, as were the radio serials that inspired them; serialized adventures—such as *Star Trek* in its film and television versions (with its prime-time, action-packed ads for submarine sandwiches, rental trucks, action

movies, men's deodorant, and the U.S. Army)[11] and serial fictions such as
Patrick O'Brian's Aubrey-Maturin novels (which a number of people have
told me they either bought or received as Father's Day gifts) are directed
at readers who are not effeminate. Hayward argues that the stereotypes
dictating that soap opera audiences are female and action-adventure audiences (for example, the readership of the *Terry and the Pirates* comic strip)
are male "can and should be challenged"; she points out that 31 percent
of fan letters to the creator of *Terry* were from women, and that "one-third
of the soap opera audience is now male" (19). For my purposes, though,
the sex of the actual audience is less important than the gendering of the
text's address. O'Brian's text, like *Terry and the Pirates,* establishes the
affective patterns associated with antieffeminate feeling, whether in men
or in women. A comparison of O'Brian's serial practice with Trollope's,
then, can offer a glimpse at the difference between a mixed-gendered and
a gender-specific technology of feeling. Taking the feelings invoked and
structured by a Trollopian serial as a baseline, I will point to the O'Brian
novels' divergences from that baseline as an index of what "masculinity"
feels like in contemporary culture.

If the characteristic feelings invoked by the sentimental text that marks
its reader's body as effeminate are the tightness in the throat and the wetness in the eye that presage crying, then the antieffeminate corollary in
this culture would be the pounding heart, the quick breathing, and the
mild sweating experienced by the engaged audience of the action-
adventure story. Women and men, of course, can experience both sets of
sensations, and even can feel them in the course of responding to one and
the same text. But just as "women's weepies" invoke familiar formulas to
bring on the "good cry" in audiences that are coded as effeminate, antieffeminate serials like O'Brian's repeatedly put their readers through the
paces of the programmed "thrill." As I have been arguing, though, serial
form sets that thrill into alternation and opposition with the boredom (or
the calm) built into the formal features of the medium. Just as the good-
cry text encourages its engaged reader to rehearse (rather than purge)
effeminate emotion through tears, the antieffeminate serial moves its
readers' bodies to a state of "manly feelings," that is, of the thrill of adventure offset and undercut by the containment of feeling the serial form
automatically affords. Antieffeminate serials enforce and reinforce that
ambivalent state of feeling and not-feeling understood as "masculinity" in
this culture.

O'Brian's twenty novels constitute a serial presenting the exploits in the
Napoleonic Wars of a British naval captain, Jack Aubrey, and his best
friend and ship's surgeon, Stephen Maturin, who happens also to be a

secret government agent. O'Brian takes great pains to imitate Regency prose style and to reproduce early-nineteenth-century nautical and social life in detail, but—formally speaking—his texts are a curious mixture of the nineteenth-century serial and the modernist novel. O'Brian's novels revert in many ways to the literary history of the century their fiction represents: in their serial aspect they refer to Trollope's formal practice, and in their subject matter they feature certain elusive corners of Jane Austen's world. With only brief glimpses of the life that women lead on the English shore, the first volume, *Master and Commander,* for instance, reads as if it were the narrative of how Frederick Wentworth, the hero of Austen's last novel, spent those seven years at sea that made him rich and successful. The naval world of men's experience, utterly unnarratable in *Persuasion,* forms the substance of O'Brian's. The novels are modernist in the elliptical and allusive nature of many of their scenes, the pacing of scenic shifts, and what Victorians would have called the "coarseness" of much of their violent and sexual subject matter; they also appear to be modernist—read individually—for their resistance of the marriage plot and for the general open-endedness of the narrative of each volume. Considered in light of Trollopian serial form, however, their particular way of resisting closure seems to me to represent less a modernist than a masculinist impulse. I see this in terms of how they handle the serial modes of virtual time (through narrative closure) and virtual space (through setting).

If Trollope's serial form keeps the marriage-plot momentum continually pushing forward through virtual time, O'Brian's resists closing it by causing the storyline repeatedly to circle back upon itself. Instead of a forward-driving impulse toward heterosexual consummation, O'Brian's novels move in a closed circle, as the protagonists oscillate between their desire to couple up with women and their desire to be out at sea. To read this serial is to be continually tossed between those two narrative trajectories, the marriage plot and the adventure plot: to be reading an episode set at sea is to be conscious of the characters' longing for their women; to be reading an episode set at home is to be reminded of their anxiousness to be away again. Captain Jack Aubrey sometimes articulates this ambivalence, for instance when he remarks in *The Mauritius Command:* "I think old Jarvie was altogether wrong in saying that a sea-officer had no business to marry. . . . Yet I can see what he meant. I should not be unmarried for the world, you know; no, not for a flag [i.e., an admiralty]; but you cannot conceive how my mind has been going back to Ashgrove Cottage these days, when I should be thinking about getting the squadron to sea" (204). Tied as the narrative is to Jack's and Stephen's states of mind, the novel reflects Jack's preoccupation. And yet, at the novel's beginning, when Stephen had asked Jack how he would react to a commission taking him away from Ashgrove Cottage, his connubial home, his reply had been "I should kiss the messenger" (32). This ambivalent structure of feeling breeds a restless dissatisfaction that never reaches the affective apotheosis of that marriage plot which settles—even with all its discontents—the closure of Trollope's novels.

Domestic space—the Jane Austen world to which O'Brian's middle-class women are strictly relegated—is utterly antithetical to life at sea. Hence, any overtly effeminate presence is absent from the first volume of the series. Like Frederick Wentworth, Captain Aubrey cannot tolerate having either respectable women or prostitutes on board his ship (he hesitates even to allow working-class women to be there as companions to their husbands, and he sulks when he has to take female prisoners on board); female presences and feminine influences are rare in the nautical world of the series. There are no middle-class female characters, hence no heterosexual love interest in *Master and Commander*, though the master on board Jack Aubrey's ship nurses a romantic passion for his physically beautiful and heroically capable captain.[12] The overt plot of the antieffeminate serial, however, refuses to traffic in such matters. The narrative trajectory of *Master and Commander* is dictated entirely by exploits of war; there is no marriage plot, and the master's desires are so peripheral to the main action as not to enter into the resolution at novel's end.

The relationship that centers the series—the only relationship that really matters in the continuing thread of the narrative—is the friendship between Jack and Stephen. As one devoted O'Brian fan tells me, reading this genre of serial fiction is "a buddy thing: as a reader, you want to like both these characters, to be their buddy, and when you see that they like each other so much, it makes you like each of them better." Serial form allows, or even requires, the narrator to repeat in each volume the parameters of this important pairing, to give the necessary background to any uninitiated reader who picks up a novel out of sequence. As in Trollope's novels, these recapitulations also serve a function for the initiated reader, as they select the salient details from hundreds of pages of incidents involving the two men, therefore offering a preferred interpretation of their friendship. A typical example of this interpretive mode of recapitulation occurs in the eighth volume of the series, *The Ionian Mission:*

> So far Jack had been unusually lucky in this respect. From his first command he had nearly always sailed with Stephen Maturin, and it had proved the happiest arrangement. As her surgeon, Dr. Maturin was very much part of the ship, having his own independent function and being one no more

than nominally subject to the captain; but since he was not an executive officer their intimacy caused no jealousy or ill-feeling in the wardroom: and although he and Jack Aubrey were almost as unlike as men could be, unlike in nationality, religion, education, size, shape, profession, habit of mind, they were united in a deep love of music, and many and many an evening had they played together, violin answering cello or both singing together far into the night. (154)

The vocabulary that constitutes this account suggests the language of romantic attachment: "intimacy," "jealousy," "united in a deep love," "together far into the night," but of course the phrases that connect these terms to form the paragraph serve to cancel out the implications of something more than friendship between the captain and the surgeon. That friendship is, as the O'Brian fan tells me, "key," because the attachment between the two men forms the substance of the devoted reader's attachment to each of them and to their continuing story.

Jack and Stephen's friendship serves an important narrative function, too, because the conversations between them (uninhibited, as the passage suggests, by any significant distinction of military rank between them) become the novel's vehicle for explaining the nautical action, as Jack patiently explains it to Stephen, who seems perpetually to know even less about military tactics and shipboard arrangements than even the most naive of readers. Stephen is the "ficelle," to use Henry James's term, who allows Jack to articulate thoughts his own consciousness would hardly need to register, for the benefit not just of Stephen but also of the reader who is necessarily ignorant of historical detail and of the fictive situation. Although the repeated summaries of what matters in the connection between the two central characters sometimes point out this function (calling Stephen a "godsend" to his shipmates, in *The Mauritius Command* [317], because his questions to Jack allow others on board the ship to overhear explanations they would otherwise never receive), the recapitulations insist on defining this relationship as an antieffeminate paradise of feeling between two men, explicitly "dear" to each other but never "intimate" in the intensely intersubjective way that sexual partners in marriage-plot novels generally are. This relationship has its limits, its explicitly homosocial (never homosexual) parameters; in that respect, it reflects that "male sort of loneliness" Ellen Ullman (1996) sees in the culture of engineers.

Explicitly romantic relationships do not enter the main plot of the serial until the second volume, *Post Captain,* where the early chapters place Jack and Stephen in a rented English country house, perfectly situated—

in classic Trollopian form—to lead to forming attachments with two young women living nearby. Jack falls in love with the virginal but plucky Sophie; Stephen conceives an obsessive passion for Diana, her sexy, widowed cousin. The nascent marriage plots of the second volume do not begin to reach closure, however, until the end of the third novel, *HMS Surprise,* where—in a typical serial twist at the last minute—Stephen, who has begun to think Diana will accept his proposal, loses her but Jack and Sophie—previously estranged—agree to marry. Jack's happy ending faces a pretty dramatic anticlimax in the beginning of the next volume, *The Mauritius Command,* which opens on the scene of his utter domestic discomfiture at home with his wife, her shrewish mother, their twin daughters, a young niece, and a series of incompetent female maids, living in a small house on meager means. Stephen comes to rescue Jack from this female-dominated hell by handing him his next commission, setting into motion once again that perpetual alternation between the heroes' desire to be at home and their desire to get back to sea. Meanwhile, Stephen's pursuit of Diana continues through volumes four and five, coming to a definitively anticlimactic resolution at the end of the seventh novel, *The Surgeon's Mate,* where Stephen wins Diana's hand in marriage just at the moment when he realizes he has lost the obsessive passion for her that he had been nursing throughout the past five volumes. None of those seven first books in the series, then, employs anything like a traditional marriage-plot closure: even those two that do end with marriages seriously undercut the narrative resolution that the ending would traditionally imply, the promise (however problematic it may be) of an intimate connubial connection between two persons whose lonesomeness is to be addressed and ameliorated by their union, a connection that is supposed to carry on beyond the boundaries of the virtual time represented in the fiction. The only such connection Jack and Stephen can count on is the connection they have with each other, and that relationship is—as I have said—strictly circumscribed as being only so intimate, so loving, as friendship between two men in a heterocentric fictive world can be.

Antieffeminate serials that they are, these novels are not, of course, primarily about love and marriage—those are only subplots, subordinated to the nautical and military feats of the heroes. The scenes that would evoke the pounding heart, the rapid breath, and sweating brow in the body of the avid reader are sometimes battles between ships, sometimes impending disasters at sea, and sometimes incidents of intrigue brought on by Stephen's involvement in Britain's secret service. In volume 6, *The Fortune of War,* Jack and Stephen debate the relative merits of love stories and action-adventure stories for moving readers to states of high feeling, in a

passage that brings my own concerns with the affective properties of novels to the surface of O'Brian's text. Jack responds to another officer's assertion that love stories are the most moving of novels because they raise
"your blood, your spirits, your whole being, to the highest pitch." Jack
counters, "As for raising your spirits to the highest pitch, what do you say
about hunting, or playing for high stakes? What do you say about war,
about going into action?" Stephen concurs with Jack, expressing the difficulty with rendering action-adventure feelings, as opposed to marriage-
plot feelings, in narrative:

> Perhaps full war, martial war, may wind even more emotions to the break-
> ing-point—the social emotions of comradeship, extreme joint endeavour,
> even patriotism and selfless devotion may be involved; and glory rather
> than a humid bed may be the aim. The stakes are perhaps higher still [in
> war than in love], since physical annihilation accompanies defeat. But how
> is this to be encompassed in a book? In a venereal engagement between a
> man and a woman the events occur in turn, in a sequence of time; each can
> be described as it arises. Whereas in a martial contest so many things hap-
> pen at once, that even the ablest hand must despair of drawing the appear-
> ance of a serial thread from the confusion. (53–54)

Stephen's reasoning draws even stricter lines than I see between the genres of effeminate and antieffeminate serial fiction. Representation of what
he so infelicitously calls "a venereal engagement between a man and a
woman" might be every bit as elusive as that of a battle, for if "the events
occur in turn" on some very simplistic level, surely more "things happen
at once" than the bare narrative of "events" would imply: I am thinking,
for instance, of the kind of double narrative that occurs in the scene in
Annie Hall where Alvie Singer and Annie Hall begin flirting in earnest. As
each character speaks in their exchange of nervous small talk, subtitles
appear on screen to convey what each is "really" thinking. Add to that the
communications they exchange through body language (representable in
film in a way that it can hardly be in written prose) and whatever "subconscious" motives the characters could be understood as having, and if
you tried to narrate the whole thing verbally, the task of "drawing the
appearance of a serial thread from the confusion" of so closely examined
an exchange between potential lovers would be difficult, indeed. The
effeminate serial genre of soap opera strives for that multiple representation in myriad ways, with its flashbacks and fantasy sequences, its
retellings of events to different characters in different situations, and its
shifting centers of sympathetic identification. The opposition that

Stephen is setting up between love plots and action plots is clear, however, and the challenge to the antieffeminate serial novelist is evident: to concoct a narrative thread out of the chaotic action that is the proper material for an adventure plot is a difficult but valuable feat. Judging by his audience's positive response to the series, this is a challenge O'Brian manages to meet, as his readers come back, volume after volume, to experience more of the feelings his adventure plots evoke.

Like O'Brian's marriage plots, the adventure plots, too, tend to resist closure: even though one novel might reveal whether the ship survived the storm, whether the British navy defeated the foe, or whether our heroes escaped the clutches of their many vindictive adversaries, often the reader has to wait for the next volume to learn what the short-term consequences of Jack and Stephen's latest exploit will be (whether they will get reprimands or promotions; whether they will see their families again; whether they will get rich from their prizes or lose everything to their creditors; whether their long-term antagonists will avenge their most recent victories; whether there will be another ship, another command, another adventure, another volume in the series). The open-endedness of each volume's conclusion gestures toward the serial nature of the project, toward the likelihood that there will be, God and O'Brian (and W. W. Norton & Company) willing, another installment in a year or two (or at least that there would have been, until O'Brian's death early in the year 2000). Within each novel's plot, however, that circular pull toward home and away from home, toward the sea and away from the sea, guarantees that nothing like closure can ever be accomplished within the series. It means not only that the O'Brian fan can look forward to a continual series of episodes that will bring on that pounding heart and that rapid breathing, but that the fan's feelings can never settle into anything like stable satisfaction with the characters' situations. Thrill and ambivalence: these are the feelings driving the antieffeminate serial form.

O'Brian's serial form contrasts with Trollope's in its handling of virtual space, as well as its management of virtual time. Whereas Trollope's serials establish specific fictional places populated by shifting casts of characters, O'Brian's novels always highlight the experiences of the same two people, but constantly move them through different locations. This pattern is, of course, only logically consistent with the genre of adventure fiction: British sailors travel, and their exploits happen all over the imperialized world. The pattern of same people/different places contrasts with the contemporary serials I see as effeminate, such as daytime TV soaps (always located in a particular virtual space like "Pine Valley," "Bay City," "Oakdale," or even *The Bold and the Beautiful*'s fictitious "Los Angeles")

or *Tales of the City,* Armistead Maupin's wonderful six-volume newspaper
serial from the 1970s and 1980s, centered on gay, straight, and transsex-
ual life in and around a San Francisco apartment building at "28 Barbary
Lane." In effeminate serials, the place (and, by implication the community that inhabits it) is in effect the main character; the individuals moving
through it are subject to change. In the O'Brian novels, as in *Star Trek* or
the *Star Wars* film trilogy, the heroes move through various locations,
keeping the narrative focus on their individual qualities and experiences
rather than on the larger communities they may inhabit.[13] This is particularly emphasized in the O'Brian novels, where the heroes move not only
from location to location throughout the globe, but from ship to ship as
well, with each volume's naval assignment bringing them into contact
with a whole new configuration of sailors and officers, some of them
familiar from previous volumes, many of them new to the readers, if not
to the protagonists themselves. There is no feeling of being "at home" in
any specific location, as there is in Trollope's series and in the effeminate
serials; this coordinates with the circular affective trajectory of the plots—
the anxiousness to go home and the anxiousness to get away—that char-
acterizes these novels.

Of course, the gendering of feelings through serial form does not fall
neatly into easy, stereotypical dichotomies. I'm not arguing that antieffeminate serials foster individualism and effeminate serials foster community.
Antieffeminate serials like the O'Brian novels create the same kinds of
communities that daytime soap operas and Trollope's series structure for
their readers: the virtual community made up of familiar fictional characters and narrator, and the "real-world" community of other readers who
connect with one another over the fiction. The antieffeminate serial's focus
on individual fictional persons rather than communitarian places, though,
as well as its reluctance to place those individuals in the settled, intimate
relationships that adherence to marriage-plot models of closure would suggest, structures a habitual feeling of lonesomeness in readers who return to
the serial again and again over the long periods of their lives it takes to read
as many as twenty novels. In addition to the thrill, then, devoted readers
of O'Brian's novels are exercising the feelings of restless dissatisfaction, of
isolation, lonesomeness, and ambivalent self-sufficiency that partly constitute what has been coded as "masculinity" in this culture.

E-mail as an Antieffeminate Form

Reading the antieffeminate serial both reinforces and attempts to redress
that gendered form of lonesomeness, as it is both a "workout" for solidify-

ing solitary feelings and a means of entering into virtual and actual communities that would offset those feelings. In this respect, it closely resembles the e-mail correspondences that Ullman (1996) describes among antieffeminate (not necessarily male) engineers. The "male sort of loneliness" (3) she identifies is a gendered feeling performed through and facilitated by the technology of e-mail communication, experienced by individuals who are both fostering and trying to overcome their own feelings of isolation. Ullman asserts that e-mail was created for exchanges among engineers who need to maintain perfect concentration in order to do their work; for them, phone calls and personal meetings are "womanish, interrupting sort of interactions" (8). e-mail is a mode of connecting with another person, but having more control over when and how the connection takes place than in other ways of making contact. The effeminate penchant for breaking into a train of thought with a phone call or a "drop-in" visit gets short-circuited with e-mail; the engineer chooses when to check the inbox, when to hit the "respond" command. Engineers are available at their own discretion; they can set the mechanism to interrupt them when new e-mail comes in, or they can postpone receipt of their messages. If a message comes through in "real time" they can answer it in kind, or they can wait until later or even simply ignore it. Like voice mail, e-mail offers its user the option of avoiding spontaneity by postponing a reply, but unlike the ephemeral voice on the phonemail recording, e-mail textualizes the interaction, saving utterances to the hard disk for later reflection or copying them into the reply, with the recipient's interpolated comments.

As Ullman learned when she "fell in love over email" with a fellow engineer and then went out for dinner with her e-mail correspondent, the pace and the substance of keyboard communication form a potential means of connection for subjects who are in other respects "out of synch" with each other. Ullman—anxious about the encounter in the first place because, as she says, she tends to "prefer women" as sexual partners over men anyway (17), something she had not mentioned in her daily messages to this man—says she felt uncomfortable walking with her correspondent on the beach, because he would not or could not touch her, and never did adjust his stride to hers. Their two bodies could not fall into a rhythm of intimacy, a rhythm they had managed to achieve in the realm of discourse through their e-mail communication, where the receiver is always in control of how and when the message comes in. "We're lucky for the email. It gives us a channel to each other, at least, an odd intimacy, but intimacy nonetheless" (20). It is, I think a "masculine" intimacy, structured by and reinforcing the antieffeminate ethic of maintaining control, self-sufficiency, and the option of ambivalently lonesome isolation. As Ullman remarks, "For women, on-line messages constitute one kind of communication among many, one type of relationship among many. Maybe this is why there are fewer of us on-line: We already have company. For the men, their on-line messages are their relationships. They seem content in the net's single channeled-ness, relations wrapped in the envelope of technology: one man, one wire" (10).

The quotidian nature of e-mail, the way it structures one's day (turning it on in the morning, checking it at more or less regular intervals, replying immediately or postponing the answer, even turning it on in the middle of an insomniac night, to see if someone's out there, as Ullman says engineers do) is what makes it a technology of feeling; its appropriateness to and origins in the male-dominated world of engineers are what mark its structuring of feeling as antieffeminate. Serial fiction, too, structures feeling on an everyday basis; in this, and in many other respects, it resembles e-mail. E-mail and serial fiction share the sense of never quite reaching closure, as they pursue the continuing "threads" represented by the reiterated "re" line in e-mail messages and the continually produced installments of the serial. They share their status as text, and they both require solitude—and its accompanying lonesomeness—to process the texts. At the same time, they both offer a provisional solution for that lonesomeness in the easy access they provide to familiar personas (in serial fiction, where the narrator who calls the characters "our friend" functions as a kind of virtual correspondent, and in the e-mail inbox, where the textualized voices have referents in the extratextual world). E-mail and serial fiction share the tedium invoked by repetitiousness, in serial form's penchant for recapitulating plot details and in e-mail's formulaic reiteration of headers (ironically rendered in Eudora Pro's onscreen window as "blah, blah, blah . . . ") and reprinting of messages. Both are technologies available for structuring a relatively predictable emotional experience each day—but neither the developments of the serial plot nor the messages that come over the line are entirely predictable, either. Both genres inspire anticipation of the next installment; both build a rhythm of expectation and satisfaction (or disappointment) into the aficionado's daily life. And both serial fiction and e-mail happen in the same place, in that combination of real and virtual space that Ullman says she and her online lover inhabited, a place she calls "the overwhelming sensation of words, machine, imagination" (14). The machine, the technology in serial fiction as in e-mail correspondence, is not the computer or the book, but the words, the formulaically structured text.

Bending Gender and the Habits of Affect

The fact that serial form is more distinctly gendered in its twentieth-century versions than in its Victorian predecessors presents an interesting contrast to what we have learned to think about the history of gender in general. We tend to assume that Victorian culture—with its corsets and spats, its public and private spheres, its sexual double standards, and all—was more stratified by gender than contemporary culture is. Sharply drawn gender lines seem gradually to be dissolving at the twenty-first century's beginning, in fashion, in law, and even (or should I say especially?) in poststructuralist theory. But the separation of gendered technologies of feeling is, I think, a subtle and powerful means of continuing to divide effeminate and antieffeminate subjects in contemporary culture. What is different now is not that gender no longer matters or no longer exists, but that gender and sex are less strictly tied than they were in Victorian culture. Now, a man may participate in effeminate culture, a woman in antieffeminate culture, with far less risk than the Victorian gender transgressor would run: that is, a gay man or a straight man might avidly follow a daytime soap, just as a straight woman or a lesbian might love *Star Trek* or use e-mail or avidly read all of the novels in the Aubrey-Maturin series. Contemporary technologies of gendered feeling are available more broadly across sexual lines than were the gendered fashions and proscriptions of Victorian times or their twentieth-century descendants.

In theory, I believe that gender is a social and cultural construction, and that if there is anything about gender difference that is essential or determined or programmed into the body, we are in no better a position to explain or account for it now than we were a century and a half ago, when—for example—gynecologists asserted that women who used their brains too much would irrevocably shrivel up their uteruses. Now as then, the effects of cultural constructions of gender are too powerful to allow us to step outside them, to take anything like an "objective" view of what bodily gender difference might mean. As I have explained in my Introduction, I believe that our enactment of gender is to a great extent a result of more or less consciously chosen actions that do not so much express gender as constitute it. What it means to me to be an effeminate person is to enact effeminacy—nothing more, nothing less. The way I gesture with "limp wrists" while I speak, the way I widen my eyes and nod my head while listening to others, the way I cross my legs at the ankle when seated: these are not expressions of my effeminacy, they are what constitute it. To the degree that I participate in effeminate cultural forms, I am exercising and reinforcing that enactment, that constitution of gender.

Exercising my prerogative to participate in antieffeminate culture, then, to put my body through the paces of antieffeminate feeling, I did read through the first nine volumes of the Aubrey-Maturin series over the course of one academic year, and I enjoyed myself. To be sure, I found I preferred to skim most of the passages that give detailed descriptions of ships' rigging and such like, and I absolutely skipped many of the episodes that elaborate, in bloody detail, the military engagements between Jack's crew and their various enemies. I was exercising another distinctly effeminate bodily reaction: I flinched from the scenes of violence. It was easy enough, I learned, to discover the outcome of battles without imaginatively living through the gory details that must provide much of the thrill for O'Brian's sincerest fans. I found, nevertheless, many aspects of the novels to be as "gripping and vivid" (to use the language of A. S. Byatt's cover blurb, contributed, ironically enough, by a woman novelist) as admirers of O'Brian evidently find them. The espionage-adventure plot sometimes literally left me breathing hard, and certainly caused my heart to pound; often I could not put the volume down when I should have been getting to bed or to work, and I hurried to the bookstore to buy the next volumes to make sure there would be none of the enforced gap in my reading that O'Brian's original fans (and those who rely on library copies or volumes loaned by friends) have had to endure. But somehow I got bogged down in the middle of the tenth volume, *The Far Side of the World*. I put that novel down with a bookmark in it, and in the ensuing four years have never been tempted to pick it up again.

I complained of this loss of motivation for reading to the friend who got me started on the Aubrey-Maturin series, a fellow Trollope fan who is not a professional literary critic but who shares my mania for reading serially. He tells me he has noticed that the pace of O'Brian's narratives runs parallel to the pace of the heroes' voyages: when the action moves rapidly, so does the prose; when the ship is "in the doldrums," becalmed in a windless sea as it is for fully one-third of *The Far Side of the World*, or when the characters are on a stakeout, as for most of *The Ionian Mission*, the writing itself seems to slow down. My formalist attempts to locate this impression in the texture of the prose—in the length of sentences or paragraphs or the nature of the vocabulary, for instance—have proved inconclusive. But I know the feeling he is talking about, the utter boredom (to go back to Miller's word) inspired in me by the seemingly endless descriptions in the tenth volume of storm damage to the ship and how the crew repairs it, descriptions of the storms themselves, descriptions of wildlife Stephen and his naturalist friend are examining, descriptions of the various symptoms of disease that result from a ship's being becalmed, and so on. What was it that made it possible for my friend, and all the other O'Brian fans like him, to keep reading, keep pressing through the boredom to get to that next thrilling incident, that peak of action which antieffeminate serial form promises must eventually come?

For me, I suppose, the payoff of the thrill to come—the pounding heart, the quick breathing, the mild sweat—isn't compelling enough to hold me. Though my feminist principles assert that I have free access to the antieffeminate blend of feelings, the ambivalent mix of self-sufficiency and lonesome desire for connection that come with this mode of reading, and though I'm strongly drawn to the potential for community with other antieffeminate readers that conversations about the series represent, my body just isn't sufficiently into it: like the muscles of my shoulders and upper arms, that part of my affective equipment has not been exercised enough to be developed to its fullest potential. In the end I can't care enough about this virtual world devoted to antieffeminate feelings to need to find out what happens in it. The structure of its ongoing plot pulls against the feelings that have been reinforced in me by my long years of participation in effeminate fictional forms. For me, there's still more pleasure in a good cry.

CHAPTER FIVE

The Climax and the Undertow: Effeminate Intensities in Soap Opera

I have always really liked to watch soap operas. As a self-respecting feminist academic, I realize I am supposed to be ashamed to say so, but for reasons I hope this chapter will make clear, I am saying so at once. I am not using "soap opera," as do many scholars, as a portmanteau to refer to just any melodramatic serial. I mean specifically daytime dramas that develop continuous story lines, rather than being organized episodically: series that air only once, five days a week, fifty-two weeks a year, to present a continuing set of plots and subplots.[1] I am one of those people who have avidly followed many daytime and prime-time serials off and on over the years (for example, *Guiding Light; Mary Hartman, Mary Hartman;* Anthony Trollope's Palliser series on *Masterpiece Theater; Hill Street Blues; Soap; St. Elsewhere; Dallas; L. A. Law; thirtysomething;* the second, third, and fourth *Star Trek* series; *My So-called Life;* and, in its first season before it became altogether too annoying even for a serial-addict like me, *Ally McBeal*), but who have always remained loyal to one particular daytime story, in my case the CBS–Proctor and Gamble ancestor of all television soap operas, *As the World Turns,* the only one of the earliest soaps created for television (as opposed to radio) that is still being produced, and hence the longest-running TV serial in history.

In the spring of 1995, *As the World Turns* aired its ten-thousandth episode; every weekday since then, another episode appears. This particular soap came on the air in 1956, when I was one year old; my mother, who stayed home full time until I was in my twenties, watched it continuously—and, I might add, highly critically, in the negative sense of that word—until she began working outside the home in the early 1980s. Some of my earliest childhood memories of television involve Lisa, Nancy, and Bob Hughes, characters who are still central to the narratives that constitute *As the World Turns* today, and who are still played by the same actors—Eileen Fulton, Helen Wagner, and Don Hastings—who created the roles forty-six years ago.

I first began watching regularly in junior high, during the late 1960s, when what used to be called "forced busing" put my racially integrated school on so early a schedule that my girlfriends and I were home in time to watch our favorite afternoon soaps together. Throughout high school and college I followed the story in the summers, when job schedules would allow it; in graduate school during the late 1970s, after the episodes of *As the World Turns* had been extended from thirty to sixty minutes, daily viewing became one of my favorite modes of procrastination. There are, to be sure, lacunae in my day-to-day knowledge of the story line, the biggest gap being the six years I spent working toward tenure. By the time I had been promoted in the late 1980s, though, the VCR meant it was no longer necessary to be at home during the day to keep watching, and I got back into the pattern of daily viewing through "time shifting." I find myself now, at forty-six, the embodiment of the kind of viewer that Robert Allen posits in his "Reader-Oriented Poetics of Soap Opera," a walking repository of forty-five years, more or less, of continuous back-story.

Although my analysis of the structure of affect in daytime soaps begins with a first-person account of my own soap-opera viewing, I hasten to add that this chapter will not (at least not primarily) be about me. Still, I don't know how to write about affect in daytime drama without consulting my own reading experience. I am not sure how to explain the role that *As the World Turns*'s continuous story line has played in my consciousness—assuming I am addressing someone who may not have followed a narrative produced nearly every weekday over forty-five years with no reruns and no syndication—except to suppose that the characters in some people's families must provide a similar length and variety of narrative incident. Some extended families in the United States might still have the experience of daily contact with a continuously present set of friends and relatives over four decades, but I certainly do not share that experience, nor do most of the people I know. In forty-six years I have lived at thirty different addresses that I can remember (there were more in my infancy), in a total of eight states; I now live three thousand miles away from my family of origin. This peripatetic history is not, I think, entirely unusual among middle-class Americans, particularly academics. In all those places, only one set of persons has been constantly present, continually and reliably "there" no matter where: the characters who populate Oakdale, Illinois, the fictive setting of *As the World Turns*. I have sometimes watched the program in my mother's mode of angry resistance against its implausibilities; more often I have willingly suspended my disbelief within the conventions the genre sets up, and have delighted in this particular soap's fluency in those conventions. Whatever viewing position I adopt, though, I have noticed in recent years that the patterning of emotional content in the story line tends to leave its

traces on my own quotidian emotional life. For that reason—and because
I have learned from other devoted viewers that I am no more unique in this
experience than I am in the other details of effeminate American existence
I have sketched here—I am interested in analyzing the "structure of affect"
in this particular soap-opera text.

Following the precedent of much recent scholarship on soap opera
(which I will discuss below), I call the activity of soap-opera viewing
"effeminate," which is not to say that only women are doing it, as I hope
I've made clear by now. While the soap-opera audience contains men as
well as women, the genre "soap opera" carries heavily effeminate connotations in contemporary culture, as it has been marketed and addressed to
women since its early-twentieth-century radio-broadcast origins.
Scholarship on soap-opera viewing generally takes this for granted,
depicting soap viewers as predominantly female, and interpreting the
messages soap-opera plots transmit to women. Such work either narrows
its ramifications by specifying the kinds of women it describes (in terms
of class, race, sexual orientation, nationality, age, and so on) or runs the
risk of invoking a universalized "woman" whose affiliation with the codes
of femininity—and, for that matter, of effeminacy—is assumed as a
norm. I do not aspire to generalize about women as viewers of soap opera,
except to say that the cultural construction of femininity inevitably res-
onates with every woman's identity, whether she identifies with feminine
codes, rejects them, or—more likely in postmodern U.S. culture—positions herself somewhere in the middle of the sliding scale of gender affiliation.

In focusing on gender (effeminacy) rather than sex (women) in my
analysis of soap-opera viewing, I mean specifically to include those men
who are as dedicated to watching soaps as their female counterparts, and
who are, in that sense, full participants in this aspect of effeminate culture. I contend that the movement of a soap's plot structures viewers'
affective lives in much the same way as daily "box scores" do for sports
fans. I am told that any loyal follower of a team will be cheered, on a difficult day, by a strong showing in the morning paper and that even on a
pleasant day, the sports enthusiast will feel at least a little depressed when
the favorite team has floundered. The sports fan, like the soap viewer, may
be male or female, but in North American culture the enthusiasm for professional team sports is coded as antieffeminate, just as soap viewing is
coded effeminate. Both activities have an impact on the emotional experience of those who participate, and I am interested in the gendered
implications of that impact. Baseball scores are unpredictable (Isn't that
the fun of following them? If, over a period of forty-six years, a team

always won or always lost, following the scores would be so monotonous as to be pointless). The affective ups and downs accompanying this anti-effeminate pastime do not follow any identifiable pattern. Soap-opera plots, by contrast, are highly structured over the long term, and in that sense, they provide a glimpse at the affective implications of what it means to live effeminate experience in contemporary U.S. culture. Box scores and soap-opera plots are examples of what I echo Teresa de Lauretis (1987) in calling "technologies of gender."[2] To be more specific, they are technologies of gendered feeling. By identifying the structure that drives the movement of soap-opera plots, I aim to uncover part of the machinery that keeps the construct of effeminacy in operation.

I will be drawing here on the reported viewing experience of the devoted viewers I have mentioned, a fan group that meets regularly to discuss *As the World Turns* on America Online (AOL), a commercial analog to the Internet. The viewers include several dozen women and men who have watched the soap for decades, whose expressed feelings about the soap, in addition to my own, form the material for my analysis. By placing special emphasis on the experience of long-term viewing, I have found—contrary to what many researchers have assumed—that audiences' feelings are usually quite distinct from the fictive feelings being represented in the soap-opera text, but that their affective experience nevertheless follows a structure the text establishes. This structure creates a wave pattern, building to a climax followed by an undertow of feeling, continuing, as it were, forever—or at least until a particular serial gets canceled. I will argue that just as soap opera carries effeminate connotations both within and outside the academy, the ebb and flow of the wave pattern (a common enough stereotype for effeminate emotion) offers some insight into how effeminacy itself is continually structured, constructed, and reinforced within contemporary popular culture.

Who Is the "I" Who Watches Soaps?

One reason I began this chapter with a first-person assertion is that soap-opera scholars have commonly referred to the viewers of daytime serials as "them." Carol Traynor Williams points this out in *It's Time for My Story* (1992), citing Robert Allen among other influential theorists of soap who admit to watching—to be sure—for the purposes of their scholarship, but who would not classify themselves as bona fide viewers. Williams herself says that she watched twelve daytime soap operas continuously for six years while carrying out the research for her book, and the wealth of detail she cites about all the daytime plots from the 1980s suggests that this is no empty boast. Still, while she speaks as someone who watches, her perspective is not that of the longtime viewer, who—as she acknowledges—may have followed a particular story line literally for a lifetime. Williams gets an "inside view" of the production of soap-opera narratives from interviews with prominent writers of daytime serials; in another recent book, Martha Nochimson's *No End to Her* (1992), the scholar speaks from the inside position of someone who has herself been employed as a soap-opera staff writer but who speaks of female viewers as "them" or "her." The pattern repeats itself, from Tania Modleski's groundbreaking *Loving with a Vengeance* (1984)—where the scholar's detailed knowledge of current soap plots gives rise to a curious contradiction between her own professional identity and the one she assigns to soaps' viewers: housewives and women working at home—to Ellen Seiter et al.'s essay, "'Don't Treat Us Like We're So Stupid and Naive': Toward an Ethnography of Soap Opera Viewers" (1989)—where the you/us division between those who watch soaps and those who watch them watching becomes the focus of the witty title, itself a quotation from a viewer. Even Mary Ellen Brown, who acknowledges in *Soap Opera and Women's Talk* (1994) that watching soaps "opened the door for me to a world that has given me immense pleasure ever since," differentiates herself from other viewers by assigning them a higher priority than the serial holds for her: "What became important to me was not so much the plots of the various daytime soaps but who else watched them" (x). For all the insight that such projects have to offer on the history, conventions, interpretation, and reception of the genre, they construct the perspective of longtime viewers of soap operas as "other"—and therefore, academically speaking, as marginal—in opposition to the scholarly perspective that centers each study.

Charlotte Brunsdon has attributed the we/they structure of so much feminist commentary on television genres to a shift within feminist media criticism itself, from a position outside the academy (where the commentators of the 1960s envisioned a "transparent" relation between themselves and the female viewers about whom and for whom they were writing) to an institutionally entrenched "hegemonic/recruiting" position typified by such influential books as Modleski's. As Brunsdon explains, "The construction of feminist identity through this relation involves the differentiation of the feminist from her other, the ordinary woman, the housewife, the woman she might have become, but at the same time, a compulsive engagement with this figure. The position is often profoundly contradictory, involving both the repudiation and defence of traditional femininity" ("Identity in Feminist Television Criticism" [1993], 313). In scholarship of this kind, Brunsdon remarks, "The pronouns . . . are 'we' and 'they,' with the shifting referent of the 'we' being both 'feminists' and 'women,' although the 'they' is always 'women' " (315). Brunsdon theorizes a third moment in feminist television criticism—characterized by Christine Geraghty's 1990 book, *Women and Soap Opera*—where poststructuralist and postmodern self-consciousness about identity positioning lead to a less stable relation between the theorist and the audience: "Everyone here is an other—and there are no pronouns beyond the 'I'" (316). As Brunsdon asserts, the history of feminist television criticism means "We now have gendered genres, and we also have gendered audiences" (311). One might add that we also have gendered scholars. Since the "gendering" of an audience or a scholar in a poststructuralist environment is no longer a question of biological sex (a question of whether viewers or authors are "women"), but rather of identity positioning (whether the address of the text, as well as the activity of viewing or writing about soaps is itself gendered "feminine"), it may be appropriate for feminist scholars to begin "speaking of soap operas" still more frankly in the first person, using a feminine-gendered "I."[3]

The academic "othering" of the longtime soap opera viewer—and the reluctance of scholars to identify themselves within that category— arises, of course, from the marginal status of the genre itself. If "we now have gendered genres" in television studies, soap must be the most effeminate of them all: Modleski cites statistics showing that 90 percent of soap viewers in the early 1980s were women, and she and other feminist theorists have shown how the multiple climaxes, the lack of closure, the constantly shifting points of view, the priority of dialogue over action, and the depictions of female power so common in daytime soaps mark them as a specifically feminine alternative to masculine narrative traditions in both high and low culture.[4] While the audience for daytime soaps may be less literally "female" today than Modleski envisioned it as being twenty years ago, viewers are engaged in a pursuit that is markedly feminine—and only obscurely feminist, in the sense that soap-opera texts continue to perpetuate such myths of the dominant culture as the primacy of the heterosexual marriage, the irrevocability of blood-ties between mothers and children, and the priority of white upper-middle-class Americans' daily concerns over those of other racial and socioeconomic groups. The persistence of patriarchal motifs can help account for the ambivalence Brunsdon identifies at the heart of so many feminist projects on the subject, "the paradox that, on the one hand, there is a perceived incompatibility between feminism and soap opera, but, on the other, it is arguably feminist interest that has transformed soap opera into a very fashionable field for academic inquiry" ("The Role of Soap Opera in the

Development of Feminist Television," 50). Feminist recuperations of soap opera have most recently relied upon explications of how viewers use those texts for feminist ends: to satisfy unconscious drives toward female power (as Nochimson hypothesizes), to serve as the focus for communities of friends or coworkers whose conversations about the plots can be critical (as in Dorothy Hobson's work) or carnivalesque (as in Mary Ellen Brown's), and hence subversive of the plots' apparent ideologies. What has not been discussed is one of the subjects most marginalized in all of academic discourse, including feminism: what does it *feel* like to follow a soap opera over a period of many years, and how might those feelings inflect the experience of longtime viewers? Given that daytime soap opera's eternal serial structure makes it a unique television genre, and given that, as Brunsdon puts it in "Soap Opera in Feminist Television Discourse," "the connotational femininity of the genre remains overwhelming" (58), an investigation of soaps' relation to feelings can provide some insight on contemporary constructions of what femininity itself "feels like."

Intensities and Long-Term Viewing

I have said that this chapter is not, or at least not primarily, about me, and—in the spirit of Brunsdon's scrutiny of identity positioning in feminist criticism—I would like to establish a theoretical framework for making that claim. The issue of television's affective properties is certainly not peculiar to my case. According to Lynne Joyrich (1991–92), academic critics of television are always anxious about the medium's impact upon viewers' emotions, though scholars argue for two opposite models of what that impact might be. "On the one hand," Joyrich explains, "commentators complain of television's evacuation of emotion" or "emphasize the 'anesthetizing' and narcotic quality of TV"; "on the other hand, many people condemn television for its constant menu of sentimental and sensational drivel, for its arousal of extreme emotional states" (26). Television criticism evinces two fears: "that television deprives us of affect (as it emotes in our place) or that TV encourages an excessive emotionalism (as we're drawn into its flow)" (27). In the course of going on to develop other matters, Joyrich suggests a reconsideration of television and emotion in terms of postmodernity, and summarizes Jameson: "Although the traditional way of speaking of emotions as the revelation of some inner core no longer seems to apply to current constructions of identity, artificially-induced manifestations of emotional material" (what Jameson calls "intensities" so as to distinguish them from older conceptions of centered and self-expressed feelings) are exhibited to us by the culture (29).

Joyrich does not go into any detail on particular television genres in her useful critique of TV scholarship, but I want to direct her point back at the medium itself, to suggest that serialized television dramas—as a genre—neither evacuate nor arouse emotion, nor do they merely exhibit it: I want to argue that serial form structures the affective response of initiated viewers, although that response is never identical to the "feelings" being reproduced by the serial text. Even though Jameson (1991) elaborates the point in the context of his argument that affect is "waning in postmodern culture" (12), his concept of "intensities" (borrowed, he says, from Lyotard) is nevertheless useful here, as it provides an alternative to traditional modernist assumptions that some emotions are "genuine" and some are "false." Jameson says that intensities, detached from the concept of a unified self, are "free floating and impersonal" in postmodern culture (16). They exist in a culture where the "depth models" of high modernism no longer operate, among them the "dialectical one of essence and appearance," the "Freudian model of latent and manifest, or of repression," and the "existential model of authenticity and inauthenticity" (12). If there is, in postmodern culture, no essential, latent, authentic unified self, there can be no personal repository of "real" emotions to be expressed, drained, or inspired. This notion of the free floating-ness and impersonality of affect suggests that intensities, unlike "emotions," exist in a state of detachment from individual persons or even texts: it implies that they are forms or structures operating within culture. My project, then, is not to provide a confessional account of how I feel about soaps, but rather to do a narratological analysis of the structures of affect in the narrative form of daytime television soap opera in order to describe how those patterns operate to structure (not drain, not reproduce) viewers' intensities.

I will not dwell here upon all the scholarly work that has already been done on how soap operas represent feeling (projects like Modleski's [1984] and Nochimson's [1992], for example), nor the sociologically and psychologically based work on what motivates actual viewers to continue watching soaps.[5] My interest focuses on the affective properties of individual episodes within long-running series. I begin with the assumption that an uninitiated viewer who tunes in to a single episode of a soap opera will be distanced from the emotions being represented on screen (a fact overlooked by much of the criticism of melodramatic forms, but emphasized by Allen and Traynor Williams). I like Allen's terminological distinction between the "naive" viewer (not, as criticism of popular culture traditionally had it, the person who believes the soap characters are real people, but rather the viewer who tunes into a soap episode for the first time, having no idea about the context of the events being represented) and the "experienced" viewer (who knows the backstory). As Allen explains, the naive viewer can only read syntagmatically, from event to event, whereas the experienced viewer performs a paradigmatic reading, recognizing the patterning among events that unfold over the long term (*Speaking of Soap Operas,* 70). The experienced viewer attains a level of literacy in soap-opera convention that makes it possible to interpret the broad strokes of an episode of a soap he or she has never seen before; approaching one of his or her "own" soaps, the experienced viewer has the competency needed to fill in the gaps that necessarily occur in the daily diegesis. Occupying the reading position of the experienced viewer means being able to interpret the unspoken aspects of the soap opera narrative: the long looks and enigmatic remarks exchanged between characters, the double takes, the pauses in dialogue, and the seemingly arbitrary cutting off of scenes upon certain characters' entrances.

The more a viewer knows about what has happened before in the series (or what is happening "outside" the series, as reported in soap-opera magazines or on Internet gossip boards), the more capable that viewer will be of interpreting and participating in the intensities being constructed in any given episode. How much you could sympathize in the fall of 1994, for instance, with Emily's desperate attempts to interfere with Samantha's affair with Craig so that she might become romantically involved with Craig herself will depend on how long you have watched *As the World Turns:* for six days? you might read her as merely scheming and manipulating, supremely self-centered, in obvious evil opposition to the devoted Samantha; for six months? you might remember the trauma of her having lost her fiancé Royce in a crisis over his multiple personality disorder, and understand this as the source of her current desperation, while you may hold some lingering suspicions about the sincerity of Samantha, Royce's con-artist twin sister; for six years? you might have followed the details of Emily's fatal penchant for falling for inappropriate men who abuse her, therefore reading her desire for Craig as a positive development, and you might consider Samantha a mere arriviste; for sixteen years? you might remember that Emily had vied for Craig's love once before, using many of the same tactics against her rival, Ellie Snyder, that she is now employing against Samantha; for twenty-six years? you might recall Emily's miserable childhood with her alcoholic mother, Susan (now in recovery), and understand that as the root cause of Emily's notoriously low self-esteem; for thirty-six years? you might have no interest in Emily's story line at all, preferring to focus instead on the elder members of the Hughes family, whose story has continued over all 10,000-plus episodes. The current text sometimes drops allusions to details of backstory, so that the more recent initiate can put together the basics of the long-term plot, but the experienced viewer who has gone through the "feelings" of all those years of story will have a different relation to what is happening on the soap today. The complications inherent in longtime viewing pose serious problems for academic commentators on soap-opera plots: the scholar who watched Emily for only six days, six weeks, or even six months might draw conclusions about the two-dimensionality of the "villainess" figure that would be disputable from the perspective of someone who knows the backstory.[6]

A naive viewer—scholar or fan—who wishes to glean the benefits of experience has several means of access to some of the basic facts of the backstory. One scholarly book summarizes the main plotlines of all the major soaps, tracing the current characters to their beginnings.[7] For the viewer who might not think of consulting the library for such information, *Daytime Digest* (vol. 11, no. 4, December 1993) sold a magazine-format "History of the Soaps" on newsstands, presenting the backstory of "every current soap opera from its beginning." The account of *As the World Turns* in the 1950s and 1960s is literate and useful (one learns of Emily's beginnings, for example, in phrases such as "After the baby was born, Susan found another man she was interested in, and divorced Dan. Dan and Liz were finally able to marry, and because Susan's new husband didn't want children, Dan was given custody of their daughter, Emmy. Then tragedy struck" (36). Later in the account, the prose style deteriorates ("Craig returned without Sierra. Ready to pick up with Ellie, where they left off. Meanwhile, Brock and Emily had become an item" [46]), as complete clauses and transitions establishing causal relationships between events begin to dwindle, reflecting perhaps the increasing complexity of the developing plot as well as the evident fatigue of the copywriter and editors. For instance, a passage about the late 1980s reads: "Niles and Jeff Dolan, a cop, planned to kill Lily. Jeff lured her to a burning cottage, and Lily and Derek were supposedly inside when the cottage exploded. There was evidence that they might have escaped. Lucinda went crazy, because now both her daughters were missing. Lily was okay, but Derek had died. Paul was being tried for James' murder. Brock really was crazy about Emily and was willing to give up organized crime for her or even turn states [*sic*] evidence against his father, if his father harmed her in any way" (47). The new viewer of the soap in search of a more nuanced account of the relationships that led up to the current story lines had the opportunity in the summer of 1994 to consult a witty and detailed history written in dozens of installments by a woman who calls herself "O2B Amish" on AOL. "Amish," as other viewers who post messages to AOL about *As the*

World Turns call her, began her narrative in July 1994, when the viewers of *As the World Turns* were, as she put it, "hostage to O.J." because the Simpson trial preliminaries were preempting daily episodes of the show. When other viewers remarked on the extensiveness of her knowledge about the backstory, Amish wrote, "It's probably a comment on my first marriage, but I have notes on ATWT from 1956 to present. I think, if it's OK with you, I'll do a running history of the show that you all can copy, if you wish. . . . I remember the show from the late '50s till now & it makes it ever so much more fun" (July 13, 1994). Other viewers' responses indicated that Amish's narrative made a difference in their appreciation of the subtleties of the current story; of course, her own feelings about the characters and events are very much in evidence in Amish's summaries, and would serve as an interpretive filter for any viewer depending on Amish's history as a guide to the story's background. For example, Amish has little patience with the young heroine Lily, and always refers sardonically to Lily's travails, as in this entry from her September 1994 account of *As the World Turns* in the late 1980s: "Welcome to Lily-land in the late 80s. The arrival of Rod Landry in Luthers Corners sent a big shiver through everyone. Rod had raped cousin Iva Snyder, and she had become pregnant with darling Lily, later adopted illegally by Lucinda and Martin Guest. In a major confrontation in the Walsh stables, when Iva thought that Rod was getting ready to rape Lily, the whole truth came out. Lily was deeply appalled and ran away (a pattern begins) to Wyoming. Holden Snyder followed. (Another pattern begins.) They spent the summer happy in a small town and grew even closer. They were undeniably 'part of each other.'" Amish's narrative, strong on causality and perceptive in its recognition of the interactions between the script and such extratextual matters as the hiring of new headwriters and the firing of unpopular actors, is always marked by how she felt—or feels—about the characters. (In addition to the obvious ironies, Amish's satire comes through in the parenthetical and quoted material in the passage above, alluding to repeated motifs in the plot that viewers had been ridiculing.) This makes her text interesting reading for the experienced viewer of the soap—who may or may not agree with her interpretations (I remember the Lily/Iva/Rod Landry story line as one of the most stirring in the soap's long history, and would not speak of it in terms much more ironic than I might use in recounting, for instance, the plot of *Absalom, Absalom!*)—but not precisely a substitute for long-term viewing.

The affective impact of long-term viewing depends on matters other than knowledge of story lines, after all, matters that cannot be communicated through plot summary. The return of familiar actors reprising roles they had created years or even decades ago would be one example. When Martha Byrne—who had created the role of Lily as a child and adolescent, then left the series for several years to pursue musical comedy while her *As the World Turns* character was recast—made a well-publicized return as a twentysomething Lily, the viewers' potential anticipation of seeing Lily again (after one of her many runnings-away-from-home) was greatly enhanced.[8] This particular soap opera also uses musical themes to connect current episodes with past emotional associations, sometimes depending on viewers to recognize leitmotifs after months or even years have elapsed since the last allusion to a specific song. A memorable example for me is the use of Bonnie Raitt's "I Can't Make You Love Me," first sung by Lily in May of 1993 in a nightclub in Malta, where Holden (beginning to regret having severed their lifelong love affair when amnesia caused him to forget that they believe they are "part of each other") has traced her. Lily is sadly performing the song, evidently still grieving that she can't make the amnesiac Holden love her; she has, however, remarried since last seeing him, and the complications of their mutual and ambivalent desire for reunion were to drive a major story line for nearly two years. The scene of Lily singing Raitt's song recurred three or four times in flashbacks from Holden's point of view in the spring and summer of 1993, and he once overheard Lily trying to rehearse it during that period, but the musical theme dropped out of the diegesis until June of 1994, when a keyboard arrangement of the theme appeared, briefly and only once, on the sound-track during a scene in which Holden is finally coming to accept that Lily will remain married to her current husband. With a subtlety that might surprise soaps' detractors, the theme's reprise effected a shift in the song's point of view, from Lily's grief to Holden's, and suggested that Holden's resignation to their separation now—like Lily's, thirteen months, or approximately 280 viewing hours earlier—is permanent, or as permanent as any emotional situation can be in a form that resists closure so aggressively as daytime soap opera does. (For the record, Lily and Holden married each other for the second time in the winter of 1998, but Holden was immediately arrested and thrown into jail on a false charge of having beaten another woman; by this time, though, the "I can't make you love me" musical theme had faded from the series' textual memory.) For the experienced viewer, the affective impact of the theme's reprise could be substantial; while it can be explained to the naive viewer, he or she cannot "feel" it in the same way. Part of the appeal of following a soap opera over a long period of time is the accumulation of knowledge of those emotive details that add layers of affect to each new episode—when the writers remember to capitalize on that effect.

Obviously, detailed formal analysis of the intensities represented in and inspired by any "text" as massive and ungainly as forty-one years of daily episodes is logistically impossible; the attempts at plot summary I have quoted in this chapter (not to mention the ones I have produced) demonstrate the difficulties involved in assigning causality and conveying emotional impact in an account of anything so long-standing and complex as the text of *As the World Turns*, and such relevant matters as casting and musical themes can only be accounted for with reference to specific instances. Indeed (as, for example, the ironic tone and hilarious dismissiveness of O2B Amish's narrative indicates), the melodramatic extremity of all soap-opera story lines makes plot summaries sound laughable, even to the very viewers who are moved by the playing out of those plotlines in individual episodes. I therefore make reference in what follows only to a narrow slice of that endless narrative that is *As the World Turns,* and I will resist resorting to plot summaries as I account for the intensities this text conveys. Taking a narratological approach, I aim to identify the patterns that constitute the structure of affect in the transaction between the experienced viewer and the soap-opera text, rather than to analyze at length specific instances of emotional intensity in the text.

In trying to locate the patterns of affect in the series, I have made "mood sketches" of twenty-six consecutive episodes from a six-week segment of the fall of 1994, looking for the interplay of types of emotion within and among episodes. I took notes on each of the twenty-six episodes, describing the action of each scene and characterizing the dominant emotion being depicted in each scene (anger, suspense, grief, sexual tension, cheerfulness, etc.). Taking each episode as a whole, I counted the number of scenes dominated by each of the moods that appeared that day, noting the emotions that dominated the hour, as well as the emotions that were secondary or tertiary to the day's main dramatic actions. I tracked the intensity of the emotions being depicted through the buildup of particular plotlines to their crisis points, and counted the number of days it took for each of the major and minor plots to reach its emotive peak. Shifting my analysis from the text to its audience, I then recorded both the content and the intensity of viewers' reactions to the details of the forward-moving plot, to determine whether the audience's emotional experience was tracking with the emotions being represented in the story.

In constructing this analysis, I have consulted—in addition to my own response—the continuing conversation about *As the World Turns* on the AOL network. The electronic bulletin board devoted to this particular soap brings together fifty or so businesspeople, homemakers, students, writers, and teachers who watch the show regularly (many of them for as long as I have), women and men who meet online to "talk" about it. This group of viewers—evidently all upper-middle-class people economically comfortable and technologically sophisticated enough to afford home computers and use them to enter the Internet—cannot be seen as "typical" of the daytime audience, because their subscriptions to AOL set them apart as having a certain degree of privilege in terms of income and educational level. While I do not wish to generalize from their remarks to make statements about the activity of all viewers in general, I am arguing that the way they (and I) follow the soap text suggests one possible mode of reception for soap operas: reading serially, over an extended period of time, while enjoying simultaneous critical and affective reactions spurred by the text.

The *As the World Turns* "family" on AOL (as its organizers call the discussion group) produces a "members' packet" including profiles of thirty-six of the regular participants. They range in age from fifteen to the early forties, with the majority being in their thirties; the group includes six men, only one of whom posts in tandem with his wife. A few profiles do not mention the longevity of the viewers' investment in this particular soap opera, but those who do reflect a long-standing commitment to watching it: only three members have followed the soap for five years or less; four have watched from five to ten years; six have watched from ten to twenty years; six from twenty to thirty; and nine of the members have watched continually for thirty to forty-one years. Not everyone who posts messages to the list has a profile in the packet, but most of the members who are profiled make regular postings. The long-term viewers are always available to answer new viewers' questions about past connections among the characters, to remark on the relative consistency of characters' behavior over the years, and to praise or to criticize the current story line in the context of the show's long history.

The ongoing conversation among these viewers puts to rest any lingering scholarly clichés about soap opera watching as a necessarily passive or naive activity.[9] They continuously critique actors' performances (complaining about phony foreign accents, bad hairstyles, or awkward acting); point out inconsistencies in the plot (drawing on details, some of which reach back for decades into the backstory); complain about the overuse of certain sets (pointing out that bed-and-breakfast rooms supposedly set in rural Illinois and in Paris are identical); denounce manifestations of racism and homophobia (criticizing the writers for breaking up an interracial marriage and supplying the African American wife with a new black love interest; organizing a protest when the producers fired an actor with AIDS); and—of course—they speculate about the psychology and motivations of the characters.[10] In this last respect, the viewers may appear to live out the cliché of soap opera fans' mistaking characters for real people (for example, they expressed something like moral outrage at Holden's neglecting his toddler son to pursue his obsession with Lily; this thread, like many others the viewers anticipate in their discussions, appeared in the discourse of the soap itself a few weeks after it appeared online). The participants in the discussion are highly aware, however, of the constructedness of the text: they share news about hirings and firings of actors and they speculate about whether the series's writers are "lurking" on the list, picking up ideas from their responses. The viewers are even competing with the writers, constructing texts of their own, including an enormous AOL file containing an alternative future for the characters of *As the World Turns,* known as "Oakdale 2," in which Emily—who had been particularly irritating some members of the list for many months—gets murdered, and many characters whose actors had long ago left the series come back. The viewers also held an online "costume party" on Halloween, for which they adopted aliases and engaged in online "chat" in the personas of the soap characters whose identities they had appropriated. The resulting parodies of characters' speech and thought patterns showed a sophisticated readerly awareness of how the soap itself is put together.

Effeminate Feeling and Soap Form

By placing the analytic record I made of six weeks of *As the World Turns* episodes next to the comments the AOL viewers made during the same period, I have come to two conclusions about the structure of affect in this daytime soap: First, the episodes follow a "wave" pattern of represented emotion, building to affective peaks that are followed by an "undertow" of reaction, and second—though the intensities expressed by the viewers follow the same wave pattern—the intensities the viewers express are not at all the same as the emotions that are being represented in the soap. To rephrase it in the critical terms that Joyrich provides: while the continuing text is clearly not "evacuating" emotion (the viewers' lively participation on the electronic bulletin board suggests otherwise), it is not "arousing excessive emotionality," either, even though it may be representing emotional excess. While the soap's patterns are structuring the affective response of the viewers, the story line is by no means dictating a particular response.

Before I analyzed and sketched the dominant emotions being represented in individual episodes over six weeks, it had been my impression that particular episodes tend to be unified around the representation of certain sets of emotions: there are anxious days, angry days, erotic days, joyous days. My analysis of all the scenes in those episodes indicates that this is generally true, that each episode is dominated by characters populating various subplots, expressing a particular subset of all the emotions available to soap-opera diegesis. What I did not anticipate is that when you flatten out the emotional impact of drawing on elaborate backstory (I mean, when you look rapidly at many episodes on a VCR in a library, over a short period of time, from a scholarly point of view), *As the World Turns* appears to represent a very limited range of emotional affect. The twenty-six episodes are dominated by the expression of angst, in the forms of worry, concern, tension, anxiety, dread, suspense, depression, and unsatisfied sexual desire, except for those episodes that function as the crisis point in a particular story line, where the dominant emotions are anger, terror, and erotic gratification.[11] The emotional wave pattern cuts across the familiar five-day pattern of a "mini-climax" on Wednesday and a "cliffhanger" on Friday, in that it seems to function within a cycle of ten to fifteen episodes: After ten days or two weeks of tension/worry/suspense/anxiety, one or more of the subplots will culminate in a crisis day of rage/terror/eros. Even the most intense of crisis days will be broken up by some brief scenes from other subplots reflecting happiness, warmth, or affection, scenes which are also always present during the days that build up to and recover from the crisis.[12]

This wave pattern contributes to the rhythm of suspense in the serial form, and results from the form's radical resistance of closure: no subplot is ever really resolved, as the undertow of emotional repercussion after the crisis keeps the pattern of affect constantly moving. In this important respect, soap opera is unique among melodramatic forms. Daniel Gerould (1978), summarizing the Russian Formalists' models of melodramatic structures, states that melodramas typically "move in tiers." As Gerould puts it: "What is characteristic for melodramatic composition is not a straight rise to the culminating point and then a lowering of tension until the conclusion, but rather a movement in tiers by which each new phase of the plot with its new 'obstacles' and 'non-resolutions' gives rise to new degrees of dramatic intensity. This new 'quality' of dramatic intensity, which builds in layers, creates heightened dramatic perception on the part of the spectator, not resolved until the final moments of the denouement" (125). The "movement in tiers" resembles the wave pattern, in that there is never a single climax to a plot, as each new complication builds more "dramatic intensity." But, whereas the stage melodrama (or its filmic and novelistic counterparts) eventually will reach "the final moments of the denouement," the soap-opera text— like the surf—never does. The intensity continues unabated, for over ten thousand episodes throughout forty-one years and more, as the spectator's "heightened dramatic perception" is never fully dissipated.

The AOL record of viewers' responses (and my own viewing experience) suggests that emotional engagement with the text follows the wave pattern produced in that text: during the periods when the plot is in the undertow of repercussions from crisis, viewers log on more often and express more vivid reactions to what is happening in the story. However, the intensities expressed are never identical to those being represented on the soap. When characters are evincing angst, viewers are typically expressing irritation, impatience, and annoyance. At crisis points, viewers say they are disappointed with outcomes or happy about them, they report that they are moved by certain scenes or left cold, but the viewers' expressed intensities are neither unanimous (there is limited agreement, even among long-term viewers, about which characters are sympathetic or attractive) nor correlated with the characters' feelings about those same outcomes. For example, Rosanna and Evan might both be upset (he is defensive and furious, she is outraged and distraught) when she ends their relationship, but most of the viewers are satisfied or even delighted to see the manipulative Evan receive his comeuppance (though some are disappointed—preferring Evan to Mike, his working-class rival for Rosanna's affections—yet resigned to the realization that the conventions of soap narrative make the young heiress's shift to the working-class lover inevitable). In short, for these viewers the soap-opera text's representation of "excessive emotionalism" inspires a response that parallels the episodes' structures of affect without mirroring them.

What does it feel like to view *As the World Turns* over the long term? Individual viewers' responses to the feelings being represented can vary, for any given fictional event, across the range from sobbing to laughing aloud, but the underlying motion of the wave pattern gives a structure to those responses that resembles the ebb and flow the culture has long associated with effeminate emotion. Even the detached response of critical irony (so typical of the AOL viewers' attitude toward the plot and so antithetical to the cultural stereotype of femininity) follows the pattern of intensities set by the soap's plotline: even viewers' ironic outrage ebbs and flows with the climaxes of the story. Any long-term soap-opera viewer whose daily mood tracks with the structure of the series is submitting, therefore, to a technology of gender, a process that patterns and reinforces what the culture assumes feminine emotion ought to be. For some viewers, the intensities are a form of background noise in a life otherwise detached from the concerns of the soap-opera plot; for others—particularly those who are moved enough by the story line to want to write about it online (or, in my case, in this chapter)—the intensities are more present, more vividly a part of daily consciousness. To watch every day is to be carried on that wave of intensities, to experience the build-up, the crisis, and the undertow of response as one of the structuring principles of daily life. To watch every day—to have your emotional life structured, however subtly, by that wave pattern—is to be continually regendered as effeminate, whether you are male or female, whether you experience the feelings as "genuine emotions" or "intensities," whether you view this process as part of the oppression of women or as an opportunity for celebrating twentieth-century, middle-class, North American effeminate experience.

When I consider the venue in which the AOL viewers' conversation is being held, I find it appropriate to think about the feelings I am discussing in terms of "intensities." Not only are these feelings, as Joyrich suggests, artificially induced, they are being expressed in a metaphorical space (for "cyberspace" is not literally a place) by entities bearing ambiguously gendered aliases rather than personal names. Sometimes a viewer will sign his or her real name; sometimes one will report that he has been ill or she is currently grieving over a divorce or the loss of a family member. When they do, a wash of intensities comes over the line: "I'm so sorry for you"; "Let us know if there's anything we can do." Do these utterances sound insincere, inauthentic, absurd? Not to me: I would say they express feelings that are structured by the conventions of Internet communication among persons who have never met, but who share certain effeminate expectations about appropriate social interaction.[13] Like the intensities inspired by the patterns of story line in soap opera, these feelings may not be "authentic" or "genuine" in the modernist sense, but they form the basis for a virtual community that exists in the absence of longtime residence in a single geographical place. As cyberspace stands in for place—as the AOL "family" stands in for bodily present persons—so do intensities for "feelings." The existence of the VCR and the electronic bulletin board make possible an extension of the family group, the college dorm crowd, or the community of coworkers who might meet "as women" to discuss soap opera. The virtual community includes men, too, in an expanded version of the gendered audience; the "intensities" being expressed in that virtual space are a feature of postmodern, ambivalent effeminacy, as potentially experienced by both sexes. These feelings are not special, unique, or original; they are, in a sense, as formulaic as the plots that inspire them. And yet we who feel them experience them as nonetheless intense.

Afterword: The Reader's Body from the Inside Out

Reading is physical; gender is performative and so are bodily feelings; repeated reading of specific pop-culture genres creates and perpetuates gendered feelings. And yet, of course, as everybody knows, this is not why popular texts get produced and circulated. The purpose of popular texts is to generate profit, to create a demand among consumers for more of the same commodity to consume. Cliffhangers sell advertising time; *As the World Turns* sells the Proctor and Gamble products it has always been produced to promote; matching, numbered jacket designs on serialized novels sell copies of books—hard-covers, even, if consumers are anxious enough to find out "what happens next" and cannot discipline themselves to wait for the cheaper paperback edition. Serial forms and sentimental texts exist for the purpose of consumption.

For many of us who live, however reluctantly, under the sway of dominant culture, of course, consumption is a mixed pleasure, always structured by ambivalent feelings of having gotten too much and of wanting still more. I experienced a vivid awareness of that ambivalence once when I woke up in the morning after having consumed the better part of a rich four-course dinner at a culinary institute, something I don't do as often as I might like to do, and hence am sensitive to the differences it makes in how I feel. I'm talking here about the physical effects of such a meal: not the ideologically motivated regret at having indulged in gluttony in a world where too many are hungry, not moralistic guilt over having consumed some hundreds of fat grams in a single meal when my internalized version of the dominant discourse says I should have kept it under two dozen grams for the day. These thoughts were at least fleetingly present, but I am focusing here on a more bodily sensation, a somatic awareness that there is a certain way your body *feels* after eating such a meal—in this particular case it was a mild dryness of the mouth, a distinct feeling in the torso, not of being overfull but of there having been just simply so much vinaigrette, so much cream sauce, so much Boursin, so much veal, so much chocolate! Having recently read Joseph Litvak's very wonderful book *Strange Gourmets* (1997), I thought of the intensely *cultural* significance of that physical feeling. A four-course French-inspired "new American" meal puts the body in a state of feeling that is part of being an affluent subject of bourgeois Western culture: I would say that state of feeling at least partly constitutes what it *is* to be such a person in this culture, as does the feeling of gnawing hunger for the active dieter or the anorexic. There's no single physical feeling that defines *the* "privileged" U.S. relation to food, but there is a definable range of feelings that are part of being a body occupying any given social place within the culture.

Reading has similar effects. Middle-class and working-class readers have often been described as "consumers" of popular culture in the economic sense of that term, but I propose shifting the denotation of "consumption" to a usage that is less metaphorical in its comparison of reading to eating. Consuming serialized fictions, for example, leaves its affective marks on physical experience; serial fiction is one of those cultural technologies that writes Western-ness, middle-classness, and gender on and through our bodies. If I can point to the cream, the butter, the cheese, the olive oil, and the chocolate that combine to create the physical effect of the four-course meal, I'd like to be able to point to the elements of popular narrative forms that make their affective mark as well. This book represents my attempt to identify those structural elements and to point to the traces of gender they leave on the bodies of their readers, and also to suggest that more self-consciousness about the ways reading marks our gendered experience would contribute to the flexibility of our individual gendered identities.

Surely the technologies of gendered feeling in contemporary popular culture go beyond fictional narratives to include such discursive forms as advice books and magazines, advertisements in print and on the air, and talk shows on television and the radio. For effeminate readers, the body's relation to such texts typically is discomfort. The dominant forms of these genres systematically structure negative feelings about the appearance of our own bodies ("I feel fat," "I feel old"), feelings constituted and rehearsed through the strongly gendered conventions of "beauty culture," such as eating, dieting (or not-eating), exercising, shopping, using cosmetics, and getting dressed. Each of these activities represents a daily opportunity for performatively obsessing over the visual aspect of living in a body, for constantly being reminded to think, "How do I look?" The clichés describing the discomfort demanded by beauty culture are still much more familiar than the late-twentieth-century attempts at deconstructing them (such as Naomi Wolf's brutally frank exposé of its physical costs to women, and Linda Kauffman's tour-de-force tracing the industry's connections to pornography): "*Il faut souffrir pour etre belle,*" for example, or Billy Crystal's classic Saturday Night Live routine, "You look mah-velous: and it's more important to look good than to feel good." Absurd as the assertion is, what makes the line funny is that—in the context of the mass media—it is so painfully true.

Most undergraduates in the early twenty-first century know how to critique the myths of youth and thinness perpetuated in television, film, and
magazines, and yet students' critical awareness of semiotic strategies does
not render them immune from the cultural pressures those mass-media
texts exert upon them. If you are lecturing on any topic to a hall of a hundred female undergraduates in the year 2002 and you happen to mention
eating disorders, you are guaranteed to be able to hear a pin drop. For
themselves or for "a friend," the majority of twenty-first-century women
students take an interest in the topic that is far from academic. Students
can be made to understand the semiotic chain linking up slenderness, sex-
iness, leisure, and "buying power," but they cannot be made immune to
its effects. Just as powerful in dominant U.S. culture as the marriage plot,
the "consuming plot"—the loosely constructed but relentlessly narrow
narrative of what the effeminate bourgeois subject wants or needs or
should have to wear or to (not) eat or to get—operates to structure quotidian activities, and not just their textual or discursive representation.
Like the other kinds of plots this book has discussed (the sentimental plot,
the marriage plot, the serialized plot), the consuming plot provides a pattern for everyday feelings. For effeminate subjects, that pattern inscribes
chronic dissatisfaction—along with its attendant anxieties—in and on
and over the body.

In contemporary culture, every effeminate subject has evidently internalized the hegemonic, objectifying gaze theorized separately by Michel
Foucault, by John Berger, and by feminist film theory. Insofar as the audience must identify with the objectifying gaze in those models, effeminate
readers and viewers are understood to identify against our own subject
positions, another source of discomfort for effeminate audiences and feminist theorists alike. Within these theories—and within my own experience of femininity—the story of the body has always been dominated by
the body's material visibility.

For most of my life as a U.S. bourgeois effeminate subject, physical
experience has been intimately connected to how I look. If I eat, my sati-
ety leads me to think about how calories will take visible shape on my
waist and hips; if I abstain from eating, hunger directs my thoughts to the
flattening of my stomach that usually follows dieting. If I exercise I am
thinking of what my gym calls "body sculpting," a visual manifestation of
an increase in strength and stamina that is no doubt good for my longevity, but secondary to the purpose of improving the way I look in clothes.
Trying on clothing, making love, moving my body through public spaces,
sitting still in private ones, my consciousness is seldom fully detached
from that question defining my effeminate subjectivity: what do I look

like? It is as if the hegemonic gaze has altogether convinced me that unless I am seen—and being seen, am not unsightly—I do not really exist.

I realized this was true for me several years ago, when I began having a monthly massage. The masseuse, a woman my mother's age, is so matter-of-fact about bodies she seems—as a newspaper columnist once remarked about her—as if she would not raise an eyebrow, even if she found you had a third leg. She works with her eyes closed, and as she works on me, I close mine. Every time, she traces the same patterns across my joints and muscles and ligaments; learning this pattern, over the years, I have come to understand the construction of my body in a completely new way. I know the place where my neck muscles join my collarbone; I am familiar with the network of ligaments and fascia in my feet. The experience of massage has made me body-conscious in a way that is entirely separate from the realm of the visual. It makes me understand my subjectivity in a mode that has nothing to do with being the object of a gaze, nor indeed with objectifying anyone else.

Just as I "forget myself" during a massage, I can also forget myself while reading. I hope the argument of *Having a Good Cry* will promote a new body-consciousness to accompany the act of reading, without falling into the discomfort of thinking about how the body looks. As I have demon-strated throughout this book, feminist narratology suggests an alternative way to think about the individual subject's position in relation to texts, reconceiving the bodily sensations of pleasure in reading and in viewing not as structured by the objectifying gaze (as they are, for instance, in Laura Mulvey's theory of spectatorship [1975]) but rather by the subjec-tively experienced narrative line, in film and in prose fiction. To redirect gender studies in an alternative trajectory from a discussion of sexuality is to move away from the concept of the self as someone else's object. In the situations of crying over a movie or getting emotionally worked up over a serial fiction, the reading subject is not in relationship with anybody else—only with a text. After all, the text has no subjectivity. The reader's body is no one's object. I believe a reading strategy that recognizes this can empower effeminate readers to step outside the objectifying gaze and experience the pleasures of the gendered reading body (not to mention the pleasures of effeminacy) more self-consciously, from the inside out.

Notes

Notes to Preface

1. These quotations and those cited in section 3, below, are extracted from students' reading journals; the quotations in section 2 come from personal E-mail correspondence. Section 4 summarizes and quotes from a telephone conversation.

Notes to Chapter 1

1. See, for instance, Robert Con Davis and Ronald Schleifer's *Contemporary Literary Criticism:* the 1994 edition collects essays on feminism by Gayatri Spivak and Donna Haraway with a piece by Paula Bennett entitled "The Pea That Duty Locks: Lesbian and Feminist-Heterosexual Readings of Emily Dickinson's Poetry" and Michael Warner's "Homo-narcissism; or, Heterosexuality" under the chapter heading, "Feminism and Gender Studies." For another textbook example of the same conflation, see the Bedford Books of St. Martin's Press Case Studies in Contemporary Criticism series. Recent entries in the series have interestingly departed from the conflation of feminism, gender studies, and sexuality studies: the *Jane Eyre,* edited by Beth Newman, contains essays categorized as feminist, psychoanalytic, deconstructionist, cultural, and Marxist criticism, but each essay pays significant enough attention to gender as a category of analysis to qualify as "feminist criticism"; Janice Carlisle's edition of *Great Expectations* distinguishes between "feminist criticism" and "gender studies," but specifies the subject of the latter as sexuality.

2. Sex, to be sure, proves irresistible as a topic, particularly for cultural studies of the body. The slippage in gender studies between the categories of gender and sexuality supports the hyperbolic claim Michel Foucault made more than two decades ago: "Surely now, we conceal from ourselves the blinding evidence, and that what is essential always eludes us, so that we must always start out once again in search of it. It is possible that where sex is concerned, the most long-winded, the most impatient of societies is our own" (33). With characteristic irony, Foucault seems to lament that all we ever talk about is sex as he embarks on the monumental *History of Sexuality* that was to inspire twenty more years of poststructuralist-historicist academic talk about that very same topic. Without in any way wishing to seem to dismiss or diminish the vast and important body of literary criticism Foucault's work has inspired, I want to observe that it is largely through his example that so much work on the body has come to be work on the sexual(ized) body.

3. Doane writes, "In the Western and detective film aggressivity or violence is internalized as narrative content. In maternal melodrama, the violence is displaced onto affect—producing tear*jerkers*. Its sentimentality is, in some respects, quite sadistic" (303). The feminine audience is, for her, in the position of the victim of violence: "Pathos, then,

is a kind of textual rape and it is understandable from this point of view that it should frequently be perceived as lacking a certain aesthetic legitimacy. . . . Insofar as the spectator is feminized through pathos (transformed into a 'masochistic girl'), the film is perceived as cheating or manipulating its viewer. The cultural denigration of the 'weepies' is complicit with an ideological notion of sexually differentiated forms of spectatorship. From this perspective, it is not at all surprising that the maternal melodrama tends to produce the uncomfortable feeling that someone has been had" (304).

4. See, for example, McRae (1996), Rothblatt (1995), and Stone (1995).

5. For an intriguing illustration of this principle, see Lee Wright's (1996) discussion of women's wearing masculine-style business suits. A masculine suit on a female body can never have the same meaning that a similarly styled suit will have on a male body, because of the history of gender and of sexual diference.

6. See, for example, the essays collected in *Cruising the Performative,* ed. Case, Brett, and Foster (1995).

7. Sedgwick shows that deconstructionists and even Austin himself eventually collapsed the distinction between the performative and the constative, recognizing "performativity" as "a property common to all utterance" (2). Butler's work nevertheless maintains the distinction, if only allusively. To be sure, the most interesting work on performativity also deconstructs the commonly held notion that a theatrical performance is an artifice, as opposed to something "real"; see, for example, Litvak (*Caught in the Act*).

8. Grosz herself moves between the figure of the body as page and the body as palimpsest: "These writing tools use various inks with different degrees of permanence, and they create textual traces that are capable of being written over, retraced, redefined, written in contradictory ways, creating out of the body text a palimpsest, a historical chronicle of prior and later traces, some of which have been effaced, others which have been emphasized, producing the body as a text which is as complicated and indeterminate as any literary manuscript. The messages of texts produced by this body writing construct bodies as networks of meaning and social significance, producing them as meaningful and functional 'subjects' within social ensembles."

9. For elaborations of the part "effeminacy" plays in gay studies, see Harris and especially Halperin's "How to Do the History of Male Homosexuality," which identifies "effeminacy" as one of four types of discourse that were eventually to be called "homosexuality." Gerstner on Minnelli provides a good example of the link between effeminacy and homosexuality in contemporary film studies.

10. See, for instance, Pearce and Quinn and other essays in the special issue of *Textual Practice* 11, no. 3 (winter 1997), devoted to effeminacy; see also the extensive work on British Romantics, especially Shelley (Clarke) and Byron (Wolfson, Dowling, Elfenbein, and Addison) and on nineteenth-century American authors (Nixon, Roberson, Graham, and Blanchard) and British novelists (Bristow, Hamilton).

11. The quotation comes from a patient of psychiatrist Peter Kramer who coined the phrase "cosmetic pharmacology" and elaborates on its implications in his *Listening to Prozac.* Kramer argues that Prozac is not a "mood brightener" (267–68), but rather something that can go "beyond treating illness to changing personality" (xviii) to the extent that "such concepts as mood, personality, and self become at once unstable and fascinating" (xix). Kramer is fully awake to the kinds of philosophical questions his argument must raise. Of a patient who had responded well to Prozac, then said she was "not myself" when taken off the drug, Kramer asks, "But who had she been all those years if not herself? Had medication somehow removed a false self and replaced it with a true one?" (19).

Concluding in the long term Prozac will be, like psychotherapy, "on balance a progressive force" (272) in culture and society, Kramer rejects the true self/false self dichotomy in favor of a more pragmatic stance on what seems to work for individual subjects.

12. In this respect contemporary psychologists contradict the usage established by William James, for whom "feelings" is a more general term than "emotions," including cognitive as well as physical experience. According to James F. Brown, "Feelings for James is the general name for all psychic states. Feelings are associated with the full span of knowledge by direct acquaintance. Ultimately this is to say that feelings are not blind. Nor are they simply physical" (109–10). Philosopher Susanne K. Langer's theoretical treatise on art, *Feeling and Form,* uses "feeling" in James's broader sense, picking up on the usage of such modernist critics as Clive Bell and Roger Fry (17, 28, 40).

13. Cognitive psychologist N. H. Frijda uses the term "feelings" to refer to "emotions that evoke a virtual action tendency, one that does not compete for precedence with other actions, either planned or in progress. . . . Nevertheless, a feeling is not necessarily experienced any less intensely than the corresponding emotion with a genuine action tendency" (summarized by Tan 1996, 75).

14. A fascinating exception to the rule that film studies tend to adopt psychoanalytic explanations for audience's emotions is Ed S. Tan's *Emotion and the Structure of Narrative Film: Film as an Emotion Machine* (1996). Tan adopts the cognitive psychological model of N. H. Frijda and the comprehensive theory of the cognitive processing of narrative film elaborated by David Bordwell. Accepting the cognitive psychologist's premise that "real" emotions can be distinguished from false ones, Tan meticulously argues that film is a "machine" or a "technology" (xi) for producing "genuine emotions." Tan considers but rejects a "common-sense" definition of "authentic emotion: a conscious, cognitive experience (such as fear, excitement), combined with a particular behavior (laughing, crying, the shivers), and certain physical reactions (such as galvanic skin responses, altered heart rate, and pupil diameter changes" (231), in favor of a "functional definition" of real, authentic, or genuine emotion (234) as theorized by Frijda and other cognitive psychologists. Tan emulates Bordwell by proposing carefully detailed theoretical models that describe the viewer's patterns of response to classical Hollywood film. Interestingly, Tan says not a word about gender in describing viewers' emotional reactions; nor does he mention the gendered connotations associated with certain emotional reactions to film, such as crying or flinching. This is no doubt attributable to his stated intention to avoid "discussion of alternative theories, such as semiology, Lacanian psychoanalysis, or ideological-critical theory" (12).

15. Modernist attitudes toward feeling also bear the mark of J.-P. Sartre's influential *Esquisse d'une théorie des émotions* (1939) and his *L'imaginaire. Psychologie phénomonologique de l'imagination* (1940), wherein he argues that a work of art, being itself imaginary, can never evoke a real emotion, but can only move the spectator to imitate the emotion the object might have invoked, had it been real. This is consistent with his argument in *The Emotions* that "Emotion is a certain way of apprehending the world" (52) or "in emotion it is the body which, directed by consciousness, changes its relations with the world in order that the world may change its qualities" (61). For Sartre, "True emotion is . . . accompanied by belief" (73). According to his phenomenology, distinctions between true emotions and merely imitative ones take on profound moral valences, adopted—as I will argue in chapter 2—by traditional proponents of the modernist aesthetic in literary criticism.

16. Lewes's periodical articles on the Victorian theater are collected in *On Actors and the Art of Acting.*

17. I am thinking, for instance, of writings that are steeped in high-academic theory, such as Alison M. Jaggar and Susan R. Bordo's collection, *Gender/Body/Knowledge,* but also of less formally scholarly work, like the beautiful collection, *Minding the Body,* ed. Patricia Foster.

18. Banta focuses her discussion of Delsarte's techniques on the meanings suggested by the poses, rather than the emotional states supposed to be brought on by the actors' postures and gestures.

19. Considering its source, Davidson's treatment of the reading process is peculiarly ahistorical. According to Davidson, "Within fictional space-time, the ahistorical out-of-time dimension of the reading process, there occurs a transubstantiation wherein the word becomes flesh, the text becomes the reader, the reader becomes the hero." Davidson attributes *Charlotte Temple's* popularity in its day to this "intimate, transformative process of reading." Having taught the novel recently to undergraduates, however, I question its ability to transcend historical differences between young readers in the 1790s and the year 2000. Davidson, famous for historicizing texts, demonstrates here the propensity of many critics for not historicizing the reading process.

20. This is true, for instance, of reader-response theory as practiced by Norman Holland and David Bleich, and, more recently, Michael Steig; Peter Brooks's theories of narrative structure and readerly response and Susan Winnett's critique of those theories; feminist revisions of and responses to these theories; and projects inspired by queer theory such as Eve Sedgwick's and Judith Roof's. See Jay Clayton's 1989 remark that in theories of narrative desire is always understood as in some sense sexual.

21. Lynne Pearce points to "an overwhelming emphasis (in psychoanalytically based film theory in particular) on reader/viewer *pleasure* to the extent that most emotions have been thought about within an economy of 'desire,' with the consequence that many others (apparently outside this economy) never get named" (416).

22. By "fans" I mean what Tan has called "the natural viewer of a particular type of film," "one whose more or less stable film preference is for that type of film and who watches such films with a set ['a certain way of looking at a film'] that is characteristic of people who watch films without any special, say, analytical purpose in mind" (11). Like Tan, I am interested in "the normal, voluntary visit to the cinema, where the viewer watches the film with an open mind, that is, nonanalytically, and generally makes no effort to escape the attraction of the fictional world portrayed on the screen" (11); with Jenkins, however, I believe it is possible simultaneously to read a film or a written text as a fan or a member of its "natural audience" and as a researcher who approaches it analytically.

23. For classic formulations of this distinction, see Genette (1979) and Chatman (1978).

24. "Formalism" is invariably set in opposition against a culturally situated criticism in histories of feminist film theory. The recent collection, *Multiple Voices in Feminist Film Criticism,* for instance, offers no defense of formalism, but supplies a range of arguments against it.

25. See Rabinowitz's 1988 essay, "Canons and Close Reading" from the *Chronicle of Higher Education,* reprinted in Richter, *Falling into Theory.*

Notes to Chapter 2

1. See Joseph Litvak's account of the conflation of spectacularized emotion and male homosexuality in *Caught in the Act.*

2. Judith Newton (1987) locates the emerging "suppression of feeling" among men in the 1860s and 1870s, "in the shape of masculine ideals which emphasize separation from women rather than appropriation of their virtues"; the ideals "devalue feeling and domesticity and valorize 'manliness' defined as 'anti-effeminacy, stiff-upper-lippery, and physical hardiness'" (134–35). Like Newton, I do not mean to claim crying as in any sense an essentially "female" activity; when I say it is effeminate, I am talking about its cultural connotations.

3. For a detailed psychoanalytic account of the masochism implied in audiences' tears, see Mary Ann Doane's excellent essay on *Stella Dallas*.

4. See, for example, Jane Tompkins's influential *Sensational Designs* (1985) and the work it inspired throughout the 1990s, particularly the essays collected by Shirley Samuels.

5. Zillmann, whose work on entertainment and emotion is prolific and influential, does make distinctions based on sex, but without consideration of gender difference that may exist within and among males and females. See his conclusions about "gender differences" in "Mood Management," 165.

6. Tompkins's foray against modernist bias is especially evident in "An Introduction to Reader-Response Criticism." As her anthology shows, Tompkins is not alone in avoiding discussion of readers' physical experience. For all reader-response theorists to date, the "reader" is a construct, primarily useful in projects whose ends are interpretive. As Steven Mailloux, for instance, explains, "Functionally within my discourse, 'the reader' is an interpretive device for literary theory, practical criticism, textual scholarship, and literary history" (192); in such studies, the reader's body is beside the point. Even those narrative theorists (such as James Phelan and Peter Rabinowitz) who posit an "actual audience" as separate from the "authorial" or "intended audience" in texts seldom refer to the bodily experience of actual readers.

7. See Kete's *Sentimental Collaboration* (Durham, N. C.: Duke University Press, 2000).

8. Michael Steig's remarkable reader-response study, *Stories of Reading* (1989), for example, attributes Steig's own crying over Charles Dickens's *Bleak House* to identification with the characters. Steig reports, "I still find my eyes filling with tears at the same old points. I have felt in the past that I must have some residue of sentimentality in my soul, and have been annoyed that Dickens manipulates me into that reaction, but that is probably unfair" (70). Steig finds the "coy" narrator, Esther Summerson, consistently irritating, "and yet at the same time I must be identifying with her strongly, on the evidence of the way my tears so easily flow." Emphasizing the intrinsically personal psychology of such identification, Steig remarks, "To get at the reasons for this will require some digging into my past" (70).

9. Davidson's account of Rowson's readership suggests that those who cried saw Charlotte as a helpless victim, her fate "not as justice but as a tragic metaphor for human pain—for the reader's pain—in all its variety" (170). I borrow the distinction between tears of "triumph" and of "defeat" from James L. Smith, who has anatomized nineteenth-century theatrical melodramas in both modes.

10. To be sure, the author of an epistolary narrative may foreshadow future diegetic events by including verbal details or patterns in the story line that will recur, even though the narrator does not, at the moment of narration, realize that they will.

11. For more details on the retrospective impact of first-person narration, see my article entitled "Double Gender/Double Genre."

Notes to Chapter 3

1. *People Weekly* ran an article about the movie's producer, Laura Ziskin, emphasizing the career compromises she makes to accommodate motherhood. *People* credits Ziskin with "fighting for" the last bit of dialogue in the movie: "Richard says, 'So what happened when he climbed the tower to rescue her?' Julia says, 'She rescued him right back!' I didn't want a movie whose message would be that some nice guy will come along and give you nice clothes and lots of money and make you happy," Ziskin explains. "Those words at the end said these people changed each other."

2. See the essays by Karol Kelley (1994), Madonne Miner (1992), and Harvey Roy Greenberg (1991) for discussions of the ways *Pretty Woman* reinscribes traditional gender roles; D. Soyini Madison (1995) adds a racially inflected perspective to her feminist reading of the film.

Notes to Chapter 4

1. Hayward's very accurate catalogue of serials' typically antirealistic formal features calls into question Hughes and Lund's dubious assertion that "The interruptions inherent in serials naturally encouraged writers to work in the primary mode of the Victorian age, realism. Reading one installment, then pausing in that story, the Victorian audience turned to their own world with much the same set of critical faculties they had used to understand the literature. And then a week or month or more later, they picked up again a continuing story to be apprehended in much the same way they had been interpreting the reality presented in newspapers and letters and by word of mouth" (11). Evidently motivated by their desire to see serials as representing the "best" literature of the Victorian era, Hughes and Lund (1991) insist on reading Victorian novels as "realistic" rather than, for instance, "sensational" (13); because of their evident anxiousness to show that serial was "a vehicle for the [Victorian] age's best literature," their otherwise informative account of Victorian serial reading does not share Hayward's enthusiasm (or mine) for the antirealist equivalents of the form in postmodern culture.

2. Jane Feuer (1986) makes this point in her discussion of network-TV genres.

3. I have in mind the kind of collective memory theorized separately by Michael Schudson (1992) and Barry Schwartz (1991), for instance.

4. A set of serial ads for New England telephone in the late 1980s followed a similar strategy, tracing the efforts of a young woman to arrange a reconciliation between her father and his estranged son through a series of telephone conversations. Rather than being parodic, however, these ads combined NETel's penchant for "tear-jerking" advertisements with the sentimental potential of serial form, and resulted in impressively effective "good-cry" texts.

5. According to Hayward (1997), "By the 1860s, magazine publication appeared to conform better to the demands of an age increasingly wishing to consume small doses of reading matter at frequent intervals and in a form enabling purchase of several kinds of entertainment at once, all for a penny or two. So while magazines and newspapers proliferated and circulations increased, by 1864 part-issue novels were virtually dead" (42–43).

6. I like Jeff Nunokawa's elegant gesture toward the physical fact of boredom in his discussion of *The Picture of Dorian Gray:* "While boredom itself can't, let us now take leave of the body for a moment to remark" (359). Though his essay frames the topic of boredom as opposed to sexual desire, one of his conclusions adapts well to an important role

boredom plays in serial fiction: "The rule of ennui readies its subject for ever new labors of commodity consumption" (370).

7. This feature of Trollope's style has long been noted: see the *Dictionary of Literary Biography* entry on Trollope, pp. 99–100.

8. For readers who aren't bored by excessive detail, I offer four more examples: (1) "There need be no pinching and scraping, no question whether a carriage would be [MS cancels "imprudent," substituting "possible"], no doubt as to the *prudence* of preserving game" (MS no. 10, chap. 20, p. 30). (2) "When he would think of this, his mind would revolt from its own desires, and he would declare to himself that his *inheritance* would come to him with a stain of blood upon it. He, indeed, would have been guiltless; but how could he take his pleasure in the shades of Belton without thinking of the tragedy which had given him the [MS cancels "inheritance," substitutes "property"]" (MS no. 10, chap. 20, p. 31). "Captain Aylmer had not the slightest objection to such [MS cancels "an arrangement," substitutes "a plan"]. Indeed, he regarded it as in all respects a wise and salutary *arrangement*" (MS no. 14, chap. 28, p. 28). Another example shows a deliberate choice to repeat for ironic effect, less vivid than the example from *The Prime Minister*, but along similar lines: "The Aylmer Park opinion [MS cancels "about," substituting "as to"] this poor woman, and [cancels "about" substituting "as to"] Clara's future conduct toward [cancels "Mary," substituting "the poor woman"] had been expressed very strongly; and Clara had as strongly resolved that she would not be guided by Aylmer Park opinions in that matter" (MS no. 13, chap. 26, pp. 28–29).

9. That last phrase substitutes for "the man she did not love and rejected him whom she did love"—a correction for characterization, I think, since Clara is represented as having "really" loved Captain Aylmer despite his unworthiness.

10. This is confirmed by Hughes and Lund (1991, 10) and Hayward (1997, 36), who mentions that the cost of installments meant working-class audiences "must often have read communally if they were to read at all" (35).

11. Each of these lists of feminine and masculine advertisements is an inventory of a single commercial break in a broadcast of a daytime soap opera and of a prime-time episode of *Star Trek: Voyager* aired in the fall of 1997: the ads for *Voyager* also included an ad for Crest toothpaste featuring an African American woman and preadolescent African American girls, with a distinctly feminine address. The ad for the U.S. Army, however, featured only images of male soldiers; the ads for deodorant and for the action movie presented male figures in fast-moving and violent situations, with lots of explosions and fire. Without making any claims for a statistically repeatable experiment, I contend that the gendering of address in these selected commercial breaks is typical of these series.

12. The novel's title seems to me to play upon something the narrator identifies as a common civilian confusion between the master—the person responsible for enforcing discipline on the ship—and captains of a certain lowly rank, who are officially designated "master and commander" of their ships. Literally, the title refers to the novel's hero, Captain Jack Aubrey, who has just attained that lowly commanding rank, but in a perversely playful way the title can be read as hinting at the homosexual fantasies about his "commander" that are embodied in the figure of the repressed gay "master" and implicit in the all-male world on board ship. Stephen Maturin's disarming habit of addressing his best friend, Jack, as "my dear"—sustained throughout the series, but much more prevalent in the early volumes—also feeds into the text's seemingly unwitting hyperconsciousness about the possibility of sexual or romantic feelings among men.

13. One way of thinking about location in *Star Trek* would be to consider the *Enterprise*

(or the space station setting of *Deep Space Nine*) to be the stable equivalent of Pine Valley or Barchester. However, the *Enterprise* (in its first- and second-generation forms) moves around in space, and its crews' adventures occur in locations throughout the galaxy. *Deep Space Nine* stays in one place, but in order to shore up the series's sagging ratings in the 1996 season, the producers added the *Reliant,* a craft the station's crew can use to travel to distant locations. This allowed for a significant revision in the series's handling of setting, as the stories were no longer centered in the single location of the space station. That is to say, the revision changed *Deep Space Nine* from a more effeminate, single-location form of serial to a more traditionally antieffeminate serial.

Notes to Chapter 5

1. As Jane Feuer (1986) has demonstrated, prime-time episodic television adopted many of the conventions of serial form during the 1980s, including "a more developmental model" allowing basic situations of episodic shows to evolve (111). Feuer sees serial and episodic form as "two different responses to television's dual ideological compulsions: the need to repeat and the need to contain" (114). Given the enormity and complexity of the story lines that develop over time, I would say that soap operas do indeed enact the compulsion to repeat, and are probably the least "contained" of all television forms.

2. As de Lauretis argues, gender is "the product of various social technologies, such as cinema, and of institutionalized discourses, epistemologies, and critical practices, as well as practices of daily life" (2), and not "a property of bodies of something originally existent in human beings" (3).

3. Robert Allen (1989) has remarked that "by conflating audience and gender address we might be obscuring important differences among audiences for types of programs as well as differences in the relationships between audience groups and the spectator positions inscribed within texts" ("Bursting Bubbles," 52).

4. See, for a more detailed analysis of soap opera's formal revision of dominant cinematic narrative models, Sandy Flitterman-Lewis's "All's Well that Doesn't End—Soap Opera and the Marriage Motif" (1988), which argues that the resolution of the marriage plot in daytime soaps functions not as a device for closure, but rather as a "knot" that introduces further complications in the story. Though Flitterman-Lewis makes no claims for the "femininity" of this formal difference, the gendered implications are striking.

5. See, for examples, the work done in the mid- to late 1980s by such researchers as Alexander (1985), Compesi (1980), Kielwasser and Wolf (1989), and Rubin and Perse (1987), as well as Hobson (1989), Mary Ellen Brown, and Seiter et al. (1989).

6. This problem for scholars occurs in the opposite direction, too, in that pronouncements about a particular soap's plot—or the ideologies it tends to uphold—may be undermined by future developments in the story. For example, see Rittenhouse (1992), whose generalizations about the nuclear family on *As the World Turns* do not hold up in the light of events on the soap since 1992.

7. Marilyn Matelski's (1988) book contains these summaries in addition to a history of the production of soaps since radio days.

8. For an interesting analysis of the semiotics of recasting in soap opera with special reference to Meg Ryan in *As the World Turns,* see Jeremy G. Butler (1995).

9. Indeed, Dorothy Hobson's (1989) interviews with regular soap viewers have already established that "the process of watching soap operas is in no way a passive operation and it continues after the viewing time and is extended into other areas of everyday life" (150);

Louise Spence (1995), too, argues that "feelings for a character are certainly other than simply feeling at one with that character; they involve both psychological processes and critical ones" (189).

Recent work on the electronic bulletin-board (EBB) discussion of television serials has begun to characterize the activity of viewers who participate in such discussions. Nancy Baym (1995) says such EBBs "provide information about what has happened and what will happen on the shows, to interpret the shows, to negotiate private issues in a public space, and to sustain relationships" (147) among daytime soap-opera viewers; Denise Bielby and C. Lee Harrington (1994) observe similar phenomena among viewers who post to EBBs devoted to prime-time serials.

10. Hobson's subjects "discuss the events on television in relation to the fiction, the accuracy of the fictional representation, and also in relation to criteria within the 'real world'" (167). The AOL group's preoccupation with the production and political implications of the soap adds extra dimensions to what Hobson observed.

11. A longtime viewer of *All My Children* tells me that this particular configuration of dominant emotions, especially the emphasis on worry and anxiety, is peculiar to *As the World Turns,* and that he believes other soaps have different dominant emotions. To test the wave pattern against another daytime soap, a critic would need to have access to the affective response generated by decades of backstory, as well as the reports of other viewers in a forum such as AOL; I would be very interested in the results of such an inquiry.

12. In the 1994–95 season, the wave pattern was continually interrupted by the O. J. Simpson murder trial's preempting of episodes, which varied by region. CBS's spokesperson assured me "you won't miss anything" when I called in January of 1995 to ask about the network's preemption policy; they had resolved to postpone entire episodes but not to interrupt episodes in progress. Local networks had policies of their own. This meant that the usual pattern built around Friday "cliffhangers"—not to mention the emotional impact of following a daily diegesis—was frequently disrupted. The televising of the Simpson trial was also responsible, of course, for putting to rest forever the notion that events unfold more slowly on soap operas than they do in "real life."

13. Nancy Baym (1995) has demonstrated that soap-opera-centered Electronic Bulletin Boards observe less aggressive, more polite, more stereotypically feminine standards of etiquette and interaction than typical cyberspace discussion groups do (159–60). See my "The Inevitable Virtuality of Gender: Performing Femininity on and Electronic Bulletin Board for Soap Opera Fans" for an elaboration of this observation with respect to the AOL discussion of *As the World Turns.*

Bibliography

Addison, Catherine. "'Elysian and Effeminate': Byron's *The Island* as a Revisionary Text." *SEL: Studies in English Literature, 1500–1900* 35 (autumn 1995): 687–706.

Alcott, Louisa May. *Little Women.* Edited by Nina Auerbach. New York: Bantam, 1983.

Alexander, Alison. "Adolescents' Soap Opera Viewing and Relational Perceptions." *Journal of Broadcasting and Electronic Media* 29, no. 3 (summer 1985): 295–308.

Allen, Robert C. *Speaking of Soap Operas.* Chapel Hill: University of North Carolina Press, 1985.

———. "Bursting Bubbles: 'Soap Opera,' Audiences, and the Limits of Genre." In *Remote Control: Television, Audiences, and Cultural Power,* edited by Ellen Seiter, Hans Borchers, Gabriele Kreutzner, and Eva-Maria Warth, 44–55. London and New York: Routledge, 1989.

Ang, Ien. *Watching Dallas: Soap Opera and the Melodramatic Imagination.* Translated by Della Couling. London: Methuen, 1982.

Aristotle. "The Poetics." In *Criticism: The Major Statements,* 2d ed., edited by Charles Kaplan, 21–53. New York: St. Martin's Press, 1986.

Austin, J. L. *How to Do Things with Words.* Cambridge, Mass.: Harvard University Press, 1962.

Balsamo, Ann. *Technologies of the Gendered Body: Reading Cyborg Women.* Durham, N.C.: Duke University Press, 1996.

Banta, Martha. *Imaging American Women: Idea and Ideals in Cultural History.* New York: Columbia University Press, 1987.

Baym, Nancy K. "The Emergence of Community in Computer-Mediated Communication." In *Cybersociety: Computer-Mediated Communication and Community,* edited by Steven G. Jones, 138–63. Thousand Oaks, Calif.: Sage Publications, 1995.

Baym, Nina. *Woman's Fiction: A Guide to Novels by and about Women in America, 1820–1870.* Ithaca, N.Y.: Cornell University Press, 1978.

———. *Novels, Readers, and Reviewers: Responses to Fiction in Ante-bellum America.* Ithaca, N.Y.: Cornell University Press, 1984.

Bielby, Denise, and C. Lee Harrington. "Reach Out and Touch Someone: Viewers, Agency, and Audiences in the Televisual Experience." In *Viewing, Reading, Listening: Audiences and Cultural Reception,* edited by Jon Cruz and Justin Lewis, 81–100. Boulder, Colo.: Westview Press, 1994.

Blanchard, Mary W. "The Soldier and the Aesthete: Homosexuality and Popular Culture in Gilded Age America." *Journal of American Studies* 30 (1996): 25–46.

Bleich, David. *Readings and Feelings: An Introduction to Subjective Criticism.* Urbana, Ill.: National Council of Teachers of English, 1975.

Boone, Joseph. *Tradition Counter Tradition: Love and the Form of Fiction.* Chicago: University of Chicago Press, 1987.

Bordo, Susan. *Unbearable Weight: Feminism, Western Culture, and the Body*. Berkeley: University of California Press, 1993.

Breuer, Josef, and Sigmund Freud. *Studies on Hysteria (1893–1895)*. Translated and edited by James Strachey. New York: Basic Books, 1957.

Bristow, Joseph. *Effeminate England: Homoerotic Writing after 1885*. New York: Columbia University Press, 1995.

Brontë, Charlotte. *Jane Eyre*. Edited by Beth Newman. Boston and New York: Bedford Books of St. Martin's Press, 1996.

Brooks, Peter. *Reading for the Plot: Design and Intention in Narrative*. New York: Vintage Books, 1985.

Brown, James F. *Affectivity: Its Language and Meaning*. Washington, D.C.: University Press of America, 1982.

Brown, Mary Ellen. "Motley Moments: Soap Operas, Carnival, Gossip and the Power of the Utterance." In *Television and Women's Culture: The Politics of the Popular*, edited by Mary Ellen Brown, 183–98. London: Sage Publications, 1990.

———. *Soap Opera and Women's Talk: The Pleasure of Resistance*. Thousand Oaks, Calif.: Sage Publications, 1994.

Brunsdon, Charlotte. "Identity in Feminist Television Criticism." *Media, Culture and Society* 15, no. 2 (April 1993): 309–20.

———. "The Role of Soap Opera in the Development of Feminist Television Scholarship." In *To Be Continued . . . Soap Operas Around the World*, edited by Robert Allen, 49–65. London and New York: Routledge, 1995.

Butler, Jeremy G. "'I'm Not a Doctor, But I Play One on TV': Characters, Actors, and Acting in Television Soap Opera." In *To Be Continued . . . Soap Operas Around the World*, edited by Robert Allen, 145–63. London and New York: Routledge, 1995.

Butler, Judith P. *Bodies that Matter: On the Discursive Limits of "Sex."* New York: Routledge, 1993a.

———. "Imitation and Gender Insubordination." In *The Lesbian and Gay Studies Reader*, edited by Henry Abelove, Michele Barale, and David Halperin, 307–20. New York: Routledge, 1993b.

Calvino, Italo. *If on a Winter's Night a Traveler*. Translated by William Weaver. San Diego: Harcourt Brace Jovanovich, 1981.

Carson, Diane, Linda Dittmar, and Janice R. Welsch, eds. *Multiple Voices in Feminist Film Criticism*. Minneapolis: University of Minnesota Press, 1994.

Case, Sue-Ellen, Philip Brett, and Susan Leigh Foster, eds. *Cruising the Performative: Interventions into the Representation of Ethnicity, Nationality, and Sexuality*. Bloomington: Indiana University Press, 1995.

Chatman, Seymour. *Story and Discourse: Narrative Structure in Fiction and Film*. Ithaca, N.Y.: Cornell University Press, 1978.

Clarke, Eric O. "Shelley's Heart: Sexual Politics and Cultural Value." *Yale Journal of Criticism* 8 (spring 1995): 187–208.

Clayton, Jay. "Narrative and Theories of Desire." *Critical Inquiry* 16, no. 1 (autumn 1989): 33–53.

Cohen, Paula Marantz. *The Daughter as Reader: Encounters Between Literature and Life*. Ann Arbor: University of Michigan Press, 1996.

Compesi, Ronald J. "Gratifications of Daytime Serial Viewers." *Journalism Quarterly* 57 (spring 1980): 155–58.

Con Davis, Robert, and Ronald Schleifer, eds. *Contemporary Literary Criticism: Literary and Cultural Studies*. New York and London: Longmans, 1994.

Cornelius, Randolph. *The Science of Emotion: Research and Tradition in the Psychology of Emotion.* Upper Saddle River, N.J.: Prentice-Hall, 1996.

Culler, Jonathan. *On Deconstruction: Theory and Criticism after Structuralism.* Ithaca, N.Y.: Cornell University Press, 1982.

Davidson, Cathy N., ed. *Reading in America: Literature and Social History,* 157–79. Baltimore, Md.: Johns Hopkins University Press, 1989.

de Lauretis, Teresa. *Technologies of Gender: Essays on Theory, Film, and Fiction.* Bloomington: Indiana University Press, 1987.

Dickens, Charles. *Great Expectations.* Edited by Janice Carlisle. Boston: Bedford Books of St. Martin's Press, 1996.

Doane, Mary Ann. "The Moving Image: Pathos and the Maternal." In *Imitations of Life: A Reader on Film and Television Melodrama,* edited by Marcia Landy, 283–306. Detroit: Wayne State University Press, 1991.

Douglas, Ann. *The Feminization of American Culture.* New York: Knopf, 1977.

Dowling, Linda. "Esthetes and Effeminati." *Raritan* 12 (Winter 1993): 52–68.

DuCille, Ann. *The Coupling Convention: Sex, Text, and Tradition in Black Women's Fiction.* New York: Oxford University Press, 1993.

Ekman, Paul. "Expression and the Nature of Emotion." In *Approaches to Emotion,* edited by Klaus R. Scherer and Paul Ekman, 319–43. Hillsdale, N.J.: L. Erlbaum Associates, 1984.

Elfenbein, Andrew. "Byronism and the Work of Homosexual Performance in Early Victorian England." *Modern Language Quarterly* 54 (1993): 535–66.

Feuer, Jane. "Narrative Form in American Network Television." In *High Theory/ Low Culture: Analysing Popular Television and Film,* edited by Colin MacCabe, 101–14. New York: St. Martin's Press, 1986.

Fine, Marshall. "'Stella' Really Lathers up the Soap." *Burlington Free Press,* 3 February 1990, A5.

Fisher, Philip. *Hard Facts: Setting and Form in the American Novel.* New York: Oxford University Press, 1987.

Flitterman-Lewis, Sandy. "All's Well That Doesn't End: Soap Operas and the Marriage Motif." *Camera Obscura: A Journal of Feminism, Culture, and Media Studies* 16 (January 1988): 119–27.

Foster, Patricia, ed. *Minding the Body: Women Writers on Body and Soul.* New York: Doubleday, 1994.

Foucault, Michel. *The History of Sexuality.* Vol. 1. Translated by Robert Hurley. New York: Vintage Books, 1980.

Frijda, N. H. *The Emotions.* Cambridge: Cambridge University Press, 1986.

Genette, Gérard. *Narrative Discourse: An Essay in Method.* Translated by Jane E. Lewin. Ithaca, N.Y.: Cornell University Press, 1979.

Geraghty, Christine. *Women and Soap Opera.* Oxford: Polity Press, 1990.

Gerould, Daniel. "Russian Formalist Theories of Melodrama." *Journal of American Culture* 1, no. 1 (spring 1978): 152–68.

Gerstner, David. "The Production and Display of the Closet: Making Minnelli's *Tea and Sympathy.*" *Film Quarterly* 50 (spring 1997): 13–26.

Greenberg, Harvey Roy. "Re-screwed: Pretty Woman's Co-opted Feminism." *Journal of Popular Film and Television* 19, no. 1 (spring 1991): 9–13.

Grosz, Elizabeth. *Volatile Bodies: Toward a Corporeal Feminism.* Bloomington: Indiana University Press, 1994.

Halperin, David M. "How to Do the History of Male Homosexuality." *GLQ* 6 (2000): 87–123.

Hamilton, Alice. *Exploring the Dangerous Trades.* Boston: Little, Brown, and Company, 1943.

Hamilton, Lisa K. "New Women and 'Old' Men." In *Women and British Aestheticism,* edited by Talia Schaffer and Kathy Alexis Psomiades, 62–80. Charlottesville: University of Virginia Press.

Haraway, Donna J. *Simians, Cyborgs, and Women: The Reinvention of Nature.* New York: Routledge, 1991.

Harris, Daniel R. "Effeminacy." *Michigan Quarterly Review* 30 (winter 1991): 72–81.

Hayward, Jennifer. *Consuming Pleasures: Active Audiences and Serial Fictions from Dickens to Soap Opera.* Lexington: University Press of Kentucky, 1997.

Hinds, Julie. "Get Out Your Handkerchiefs." *Burlington Free Press,* 30 November 1989, D13.

Hobson, Dorothy. "Soap Operas at Work." In *Remote Control: Television, Audiences, and Cultural Power,* edited by Ellen Seiter, Hans Borchers, Gabriele Kreutzner, and Eva-Maria Warth. London and New York: Routledge, 1989.

Holland, Norman N. *The Dynamics of Literary Response.* New York: Oxford University Press, 1968.

———. *Poems in Persons: An Introduction to the Psychoanalysis of Literature.* New York: Norton, 1973.

———. *Five Readers Reading.* New Haven, Conn.: Yale University Press, 1975.

Housman, A. E. "The Name and Nature of Poetry." In *A. E. Housman: Selected Prose,* edited by John Carter, 168–95. New York: Cambridge University Press, 1961.

Hughes, Linda K., and Michael Lund. *The Victorian Serial.* Charlottesville: University Press of Virginia, 1991.

Huyssens, Andreas. "Mass Culture as Woman: Modernism's Other." In *After the Great Divide,* edited by Andreas Huyssens. Bloomington: Indiana University Press, 1986.

Izard, Carroll E. *The Face of Emotion.* New York: Appleton, Century, Crofts. 1971.

Jacobs, Naomi. Personal correspondence. 26 April 1990.

Jaggar, Alison M., and Susan R. Bordo, eds. *Gender/Body/Knowledge: Feminist Reconstructions of Being and Knowing.* New Brunswick, N.J.: Rutgers University Press, 1989.

Jameson, Frederic. *Postmodernism, or, The Cultural Logic of Late Capitalism.* Durham, N.C.: Duke University Press, 1991.

Jenkins, Henry. "'Strangers No More, We Sing': Filking and the Social Construction of the Science Fiction Fan Community." In *The Adoring Audience: Fan Culture and Popular Media,* edited by Lisa A. Lewis, 208–36. London: Routledge, 1992a.

———. *Textual Poachers: Television Fans and Participatory Culture.* New York: Routledge, 1992b.

Joyrich, Lynne. "Going through the E/Motions: Gender, Postmodernism, and Affect in Television Studies." *Discourse: Journal for Theoretical Studies in Media and Culture* 14, no. 1 (winter 1991–92): 23–40.

Kelley, Karol. "A Modern Cinderella." *Journal of American Culture* 17, no. 1 (spring 1994): 87–92.

Kelley, Mary. *Private Woman, Public Stage: Literary Domesticity in Nineteenth-Century America.* New York: Oxford University Press, 1984.

Kielwasser, Alfred P., and Michelle A. Wolf. "The Appeal of Soap Opera: An Analysis of Process and Duality in Dramatic Serial Gratifications." *Journal of Popular Culture* 23, no. 2 (fall 1989): 111–24.

Kövecses, Zoltán. *Emotion Concepts.* Berlin, Heidelberg: Springer-Verlag, 1990.

Kramer, Peter. *Listening to Prozac*. New York: Viking, 1990.

Kroll, Jack. "A 'Winter's Tale' as You Like It: Shakespeare's Alive and Well and in Bohemia." *Newsweek*, 3 April 1989, 70.

Langer, Susanne K. *Feeling and Form*. New York: Scribner, 1953.

Lewes, George Henry. *On Actors and the Art of Acting*. New York: H. Holt and Company, 1892.

Litvak, Joseph. *Caught in the Act: Theatricality in the Nineteenth-Century English Novel*. Berkeley: University of California Press, 1992.

———. *Strange Gourmets: Sophistication, Theory, and the Novel*. Durham, N.C.: Duke University Press, 1997.

Lyotard, Jean François. *The Postmodern Condition: A Report on Knowledge*. Translated by Geoff Bennington and Brian Massumi. Minneapolis: University of Minnesota Press, 1984.

Madison, D. Soyini. "Pretty Woman through the Triple Lens of Black Feminist Spectatorship." In *From Mouse to Mermaid: The Politics of Film, Gender, and Culture*, edited by Elizabeth Bell, Lynda Haas, and Laura Sells, 224–35. Bloomington: Indiana University Press, 1995.

Mailloux, Steven. *Interpretive Conventions: The Reader in the Study of American Fiction*. Ithaca, N.Y.: Cornell University Press, 1982.

Martin, Emily. *The Woman in the Body: A Cultural Analysis of Reproduction*. Boston: Beacon Press, 1990.

Matelski, Marilyn J. *The Soap Opera Evolution: America's Enduring Romance with Daytime Drama*. Jefferson, N.C.: McFarland, 1988.

Maupin, Armistead. *Tales of the City*. New York: Harper Perennial, 1994.

McRae, Shannon. "Coming Apart at the Seams: Sex, Text and the Virtual Body." In *Wired Women: Gender and New Realities in Cyberspace*, edited by Lynn Cherny and Elizabeth Reba Weise, 242–64. Seattle: Seal Press, 1996.

Miller, D. A. *Narrative and Its Discontents: Problems of Closure in the Traditional Novel*. Princeton, N.J.: Princeton University Press, 1981.

———. *The Novel and the Police*. Berkeley: University of California Press, 1988.

Miner, Madonne. "No Matter What They Say, It's All About Money." *Journal of Popular Film and Television* 20, no. 1 (spring 1992): 8–14.

Modleski, Tania. *Loving With a Vengeance: Mass Produced Fantasies for Women*. 1982. New York: Methuen, 1984.

Mulvey, Laura. "Visual Pleasure and Narrative Cinema." *Screen* 16, no. 3 (autumn 1975): 6–18.

Newton, Judith Lowder. "Making—and Remaking—History: Another Look at 'Patriarchy.'" In *Feminist Issues in Literary Scholarship*, edited by Shari Benstock, 124–40. Bloomington: Indiana University Press, 1987.

Nixon, Nicola. "Men and Coats; Or, the Politics of the Dandiacal Body in Melville's 'Benito Cereno.'" *PMLA* 114 (May 1999): 359–72.

Nochimson, Martha. *No End to Her: Soap Opera and the Female Subject*. Berkeley: University of California Press, 1992.

Nunokawa, Jeff. "The Importance of Being Bored: The Dividends of Ennui in *The Picture of Dorian Gray*." *Studies in the Novel* 28, no. 3 (fall 1996): 357–71.

Oliver, Mary Beth. "Exploring the Paradox of the Enjoyment of Sad Films." *Human Communication Research* 19, no. 3 (March 1993): 315–42.

Papashvily, Helen. *All the Happy Endings: A Study of the Domestic Novel in America, the*

Women Who Wrote It, the Women Who Read It, in the Nineteenth-Century. New York: Harper, 1956.

Pearce, Lynne. Review of *Engaging Characters: Fiction, Emotion, and the Cinema,* by Murray Smith. *Screen* 37, no. 4 (winter 1996): 415–18.

Pearce, Mary, and Vincent Quinn, eds. "Luxurious Sexualities: Effeminacy, Consumption, and the Body Politic in Eighteenth-Century Representation." Special issue of *Textual Practice* 11 (winter 1997).

People Weekly. "Laura Ziskin: Pretty Woman Was for Herself, Even If Teenage Boys Dug It. (Lights, Cameras, a Piece of the Action—Inside Hollywood! Women, Sex & Power)." Vol. 35, spring 1995, 47.

Plutchik, Robert. "A General Psychoevolutionary Theory of Emotion." In *Emotion: Theory, Research, and Experience.* Vol. 1, *Theories of Emotion,* edited by Robert Plutchik and Henry Kellerman, 3–33. New York and London: Academic Press, 1980.

———. "Emotions: A General Psychoevolutionary Theory." In *Approaches to Emotion,* edited by Klaus R. Scherer and Paul Ekman, 197–219. Hillsdale, N.J.: L. Erlbaum Associates, 1984.

Prince, Gerald. *Narratology: The Form and Functioning of Narrative.* Berlin: Mouton, 1982.

Rabinowitz, Peter J. "Canons and Close Readings." In *Falling into Theory: Conflicting Views on Reading Literature.* Compiled by David H. Richter. Boston: Bedford Books, 1994.

Rittenhouse, Gilah. "The Nuclear Family Is Alive and Well: *As The World Turns.*" In *Staying Tuned: Contemporary Soap Opera Criticism,* edited by Suzanne Frentz, 48–53. Bowling Green, Ohio: Bowling Green State University Popular Press, 1992.

Roach, Joseph. *The Player's Passion: Studies in the Science of Acting.* Newark: University of Delaware Press; London: Associated University Presses, 1985.

Roberson, Susan L. "'Degenerate Effeminacy' and the Making of a Msculine Spirituality in the Sermons of Ralph Waldo Emerson." In *Muscular Christianity: Embodying the Victorian Age,* edited by Donald E. Halk, 150–72. Cambridge, UK: Cambridge University Press.

Roof, Judith. *Come As You Are: Sexuality and Narrative.* New York: Columbia University Press, 1996.

Rothblatt, Martine. *The Apartheid of Sex: A Manifesto on the Freedom of Gender.* New York: Crown Books, 1995.

Rowson, Susanna. *Charlotte Temple.* Edited by Cathy N. Davidson. New York: Oxford University Press, 1986.

Rubin, Alan, and Elizabeth M. Perse. "Audience Activity and Soap Opera Involvement: A Uses and Effects Investigation." *Human Communication Research* 14, no. 2 (winter 1987): 246–68.

Rubin, Gayle. "Thinking Sex: Notes for a Radical Theory of the Politics of Sexuality." In *American Feminist Thought at Century's End: A Reader,* edited by Linda S. Kauffman, 3–64. Cambridge, Mass., and Oxford, UK: Blackwell, 1993.

Samuels, Shirley. *The Culture of Sentiment : Race, Gender, and Sentimentality in Nineteenth-century America.* New York: Oxford University Press, 1992.

Sartre, Jean-Paul. *L'imaginaire. Psychologie phénomonologique de l'imagination.* Paris: Gallimard, 1940.

———. *The Emotions, Outline of a Theory.* Translated by Bernard Frechtman. New York: Philosophical Library, 1948.

Schor, Naomi. *Reading in Detail: Aesthetics and the Feminine.* New York and London: Methuen, 1987.

Schudson, Michael. *Watergate in American Memory: How We Remember, Forget, and Reconstruct the Past.* New York: Basic Books, 1992.

Schwartz, Barry. "Iconography and Collective Memory: Lincoln's Image in the American Mind." *Sociological Quarterly* 32, no. 3 (fall 1991): 301–19.

Schwichtenberg, Cathy. "Reconceptualizing Gender: New Sites for Feminist Audience Research." In *Viewing, Reading, Listening: Audiences and Cultural Reception,* edited by Jon Cruz and Justin Lewis, 169–80. Boulder, Colo.: Westview Press, 1994.

Sedgwick, Eve, and Adam Frank, eds. *Epistemology of the Closet.* Berkeley: University of California Press, 1990.

———. "Queer Performativity: Henry James's *The Art of the Novel.*" *GLQ: Journal of Lesbian and Gay Studies* 1, no. 1 (1993): 1–16.

———. *Shame and Its Sisters: A Silvan Tomkins Reader.* Durham, N.C.: Duke University Press, 1995.

Seiter, Ellen, E. Borchers, G. Kreutzner, and E. Warth. "'Don't Treat Us Like We're So Stupid and Naive': Towards an Ethnography of Soap Opera Viewers." In *Remote Control: Television, Audiences and Cultural Power,* edited by Ellen Seiter, Hans Borchers, Gabriele Kreutzner, and Eva-Maria Warth, 223–47. London: Routledge, 1989.

Shattuc, Jane. "Having a Good Cry Over *The Color Purple:* The Problem of Affect and Imperialism in Feminist Theory." In *Melodrama: Stage, Picture, Screen,* edited by Jacky Bratton, Jim Cook, and Christine Gledhill, 147–56. London: British Film Institute, 1994.

Sicherman, Barbara. "Sense and Sensibility: A Case Study of Women's Reading in Late-Victorian America." In *Reading in America: Literature and Social History,* edited by Cathy N. Davidson, 201–25. Baltimore, Md.: Johns Hopkins University Press, 1989.

Smith, Herbert F. *The Popular American Novel, 1865–1920.* Boston: Twayne Publishers, 1980.

Smith, James L. *Melodrama: The Critical Idiom 28.* Edited by John D. Jump. London: Methuen, 1973.

Spence, Louise. "'They Killed Off Marlena, But She's on Another Show Now': Fantasy, Reality, and Pleasure in Watching Daytime Soap Operas." In *To Be Continued . . . Soap Operas Around the World,* edited by Robert Allen, 182–98. London and New York: Routledge, 1995.

Stebbins, Genevieve. *Delsarte System of Expression.* New York: Dance Horizons, 1977.

Steig, Michael. *Stories of Reading: Subjectivity and Literary Understanding.* Baltimore, Md.: Johns Hopkins University Press, 1989.

Stone, Allucquère Rosanne. *The War of Desire and Technology at the Close of the Mechanical Age.* Cambridge, Mass.: Massachusetts Institute of Technology Press, 1995.

Stowe, Harriet Beecher. *Uncle Tom's Cabin.* 1851–52. Edited by Ann Douglas. Harmondsworth, U.K.: Penguin, 1981.

Tan, Ed S. *Emotion and the Structure of Narrative Film: Film as an Emotion Machine.* Translated by Barbara Fasting. Mahwah, N.J.: L. Erlbaum Associates, 1996.

Tavris, Carol. *Anger: The Misunderstood Emotion.* New York: Simon and Schuster, 1982.

Taylor, Helen. *Scarlett's Women: Gone with the Wind and Its Female Fans.* New Brunswick, N.J.: Rutgers University Press, 1989.

Todd, Janet. *Sensibility: An Introduction.* London: Methuen, 1986.

Tomkins, Silvan. "Affect as the Primary Motivational System." In *Feelings and Emotions:*

The Loyola Symposium, edited by Magda B. Arnold, 101–10. New York and London: Academic Press, 1970.

———. "Affect as Amplification." In Emotion: Theory, Research, and Experience, edited by Robert Plutchik and Henry Kellerman, 141–64. New York and London: Academic Press, 1980.

———. "Affect Theory." In Approaches to Emotion, edited by Klaus R. Scherer and Paul Ekman, 163–95. Hillsdale, N.J.: L. Erlbaum Associates, 1984.

Tompkins, Jane. "Reader-Response Criticism: From Formalism to Post-Structuralism, ix–xxvi. Baltimore, Md.: Johns Hopkins University Press, 1980.

———. Sensational Designs: The Cultural Work of American Fiction: 1790–1860. New York: Oxford University Press, 1985.

———. "Me and My Shadow." In Gender & Theory: Dialogues on Feminist Criticism, edited by Linda Kauffman. Oxford: Basil Blackwell, 1989.

Torgovnick, Marianna. Closure in the Novel. Princeton, N.J.: Princeton University Press, 1981.

Trollope, Anthony. An Autobiography. London: Oxford University Press, 1961.

Ullman, Ellen. "Come In, CQ: The Body on the Wire." In Wired Women: Gender and New Realities in Cyberspace, edited by Lynn Cherny and Elizabeth Reba Weise, 3–23. Seattle: Seal Press, 1996.

Viscott, David. The Language of Feelings: The Time-and-Money Shorthand of Psychotherapy. New York: Arbor House, 1976.

Warhol, Robyn R. Gendered Interventions: Narrative Discourse in the Victorian Novel. New Brunswick, N.J.: Rutgers University Press, 1989.

———. "The Inevitable Virtuality of Gender: Performing Femininity on an Electronic Bulletin Board for Soap Opera Fans." In Virtual Gender: Fantasies of Subjectivity and Embodiment, edited by Mary Ann O'Farrell and Lynne Vallone, 91–107. Ann Arbor: University of Michigan Press, 1999.

Williams, Carol Traynor. "It's Time for My Story:" Soap Opera Sources, Structure, and Response. New York: Praeger, 1992.

Winnett, Susan. "Coming Unstrung: Women, Men, Narrative, and Principles of Pleasure." PMLA 105, no. 3 (May 1990): 505–18.

Wolfson, Susan J. "'Problem Few Dare Imitate': Sardanapalus and 'Effeminate Character.'" ELH 58 (winter 1991): 867–902.

Wright, Lee. "The Suit: A Common Bond or Defeated Purpose?" In The Gendered Object, edited by Pat Kirkham, 153–61. Manchester and New York: Manchester University Press, 1996.

Zillmann, Dolf. "Mood Management: Using Entertainment to Full Advantage." In Communication, Social Cognition, and Affect, edited by Lewis Donohew, Howard E. Sypher, and E. Tory Higgins, 147–71. Hillsdale, N.J.: L. Erlbaum Associates, 1988.

Index

The Theory and Interpretation of Narrative Series
James Phelan and Peter J. Rabinowitz, Editors

Because the series editors believe that the most significant work in narrative studies today contributes both to our knowledge of specific narratives and to our understanding of narrative in general, studies in the series typically offer interpretations of individual narratives and address significant theoretical issues underlying those interpretations. The series does not privilege any one critical perspective but is open to work from any strong theoretical position.